THE OFFICIAL

DOCTOR
WHO

AND THE

DALEKS
BOOK

THE OFFICIAL

DOCTOR WHO

AND THE

DALEKS BOOK

JOHN PEEL & TERRY NATION

ST. MARTIN'S PRESS / NEW YORK

Design by Jaye Zimet

Library of Congress Cataloging-in-Publication Data

Peel, John, 1954–
     The official Doctor Who and the Daleks book : the complete story of the Time Lord's greatest foes / John Peel and Terry Nation.
          p.   cm.
     ISBN 0-312-02264-6
     1. Doctor Who (Television program)   I. Nation, Terry.   II. Title. III. Title: Daleks book.
PN1992.77.D6273P4345 1988
791.45′72—dc19   88-18847
                                                              CIP

First Edition

10 9 8 7 6 5 4 3 2 1

FOREWORD

Doctor Who is celebrating its twenty-fifth anniversary, making it the longest-running TV science fiction series ever aired. I find it difficult to comprehend that it is a quarter of a century since the Daleks first burst into British living rooms and became, virtually overnight, superstars.

They have gone on to rack up many records and superlatives. They have been seen all over our planet. Their battlecry—"Exterminate!"—has been dubbed into countless languages. And, most important for me, they have made a place for themselves in television history.

For all these reasons and more I retain an enormous affection for the Daleks. They have rewarded me in many ways, and not least amongst these benefits have been the opportunities to meet fans all over the world. They are dedicated and wonderful people, and I am extremely grateful to all of them.

However, in this silver jubilee year, the Daleks have given me one major problem. In media interviews that enquire my age, I have maintained I am thirty-nine. Am I stretching credulity when a simple calculation reveals I must have been fourteen years old when I wrote those first episodes? Happy birthday, Daleks—long may your reign of terror continue!

—Terry Nation, 1988

ACKNOWLEDGMENTS

Special thanks are most certainly due to Jeremy and Paula Bentham, who provided much help and humor that were needed. Their Cyber Mark Services publication "Doctor Who: An Adventure in Space and Time" gave many small points of information on Dalek stories that would otherwise have been extremely difficult to track down.

Thanks also must go to Jean-Marc and Randy Lofficier; to Eric Hoffman; to Barbara Fister-Liltz; and certainly not least to Roger Hancock, our highly efficient agent, and Stuart Moore, our enthusiastic editor.

For permission to reproduce stills, we are grateful to Jon Pertwee, Mrs. Patrick Troughton, and Sue Moore.

CONTENTS

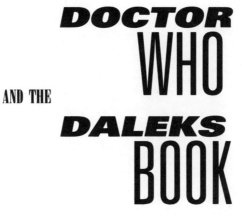

THE OFFICIAL

DOCTOR
WHO

AND THE

DALEKS
BOOK

CHAPTER 1

THE
DALEKS

AN INTRODUCTION

The *Penguin Book of Modern Quotations* contains, for an entry on Terry Nation, a single word: *exterminate.*

A whole generation of British schoolchildren grew up chanting this word in metallic tones (as best they could, at any rate). The word has come to mean one thing to the British public, even to that small segment that has never watched *Doctor Who:* the Daleks.

Everyone loves a good villain, and it would seem to be axiomatic that a hero is only as heroic as the villains he or she faces are dastardly. James Bond would hardly be a superspy if he were pitted against some penny-ante thugs shaking down a few shopkeepers for protection money. Captain Kirk and the men of the good ship *Enterprise* would hardly be popular if they spent their time in space giving out tickets for traffic violations. What would Sherlock Holmes be without Moriarty to foil? And where would Doctor Who be without the Daleks?

The early sixties were times of deep uncertainty. The specter of the mushroom cloud loomed on the horizon. British schoolchildren were watching *Doctor Who* at home, and at school they were hearing lectures called "One in Three." These were talks on how to survive a nuclear attack, estimating that only one in three would live through it. The children didn't take nuclear Armageddon all that seriously, but they took *Doctor Who* to heart. In the second story, the Doctor landed on the planet Skaro. It was a scarred planet, for it had suffered what the human race hoped to avoid: atomic annihilation.

The planet was dead—all ashes and petrified rock. A small animal had died and frozen; plants preserved their fragile beauty only until touched. This was a picture of what could happen if the politicians of the world outran whatever sense they might possess. This could have been Earth, and it wasn't hard to make that slight jump of belief. It may be modern to talk of nuclear winter as though it were some novel concept, but the Daleks showed the terrifying potential to the public twenty-five years ago. The end result of the bomb was death—not just to people, but to a world.

All looked completely dead on planet Skaro, but there were survivors—and what survivors they were. The Daleks hid in their city, confined within their machines to even live. They could no longer survive without the radiation that once would have killed them. At first, we were not shown the Daleks themselves; the most that appeared on the screen was a small, wizened claw. It wasn't hard to judge how terribly mutated they must have been, though, from the expressions on the faces of Ian and the Doctor. It was as though the show were saying to all those "One in Three" talks: "Yes, one in three can survive; but *what* will they be like if they do?"

The other survivors were the Thals—tall, graceful, beautiful people who now espoused peace as they had once served war. They were the potential, the promise, that even out of all this perhaps the human race would continue. Naturally, there was a final, cataclysmic battle with the Daleks for survival. This is the stuff that myths are woven from—the fight between Good and Evil. It was a fight for destiny, and Good, naturally, triumphed. The perverted science of the Daleks was beaten by the straightforward honesty and simplicity of the Thals. Had the story of the Daleks ended there, it would have been a fine tale, with exactly the right amount of warning and message: Beware.

However, like so many myths, the Daleks broke away from their origins. They refused to stay dead, and continual demand over twenty-five years has returned them again and again to fight against the Doctor. They lose all the battles, but they have never given up on the war. Each time the Daleks appear on the show, the ratings soar. They still appeal to something within the viewers, and they are as popular as ever they have been. In England everyone knows what a Dalek is; they can be used in cartoon strips as images and no one has to wonder what those tin-pot creations might be.

Like Sherlock Holmes, Tarzan, and James Bond, the Daleks are part of popular mythology. Oddly enough, they are not heroes, as are the others, but villains. There are not many villains that achieve the status that the Daleks have. In general villains are simply there for heroes to vanquish; they are not generally expected to take on any sort of life of their own. While *Doctor Who* himself is also accepted as an institution in England, it was always the Daleks who seemed to slip in and beat him in terms of sheer popularity. Comedy shows could parody them in the certainty that the audience would get the joke. When Dave Allen in his shows played a minister whose font turned on him, everyone knew that the font was really a Dalek. It wasn't a surprise when Allen dived into his pulpit, which vanished with the roaring sound of the *Tardis*. Rod Hull and Emu could fight savage dustbins that had invaded Earth. The children's show *Crackerjack* even borrowed a Dalek when they did a *Doctor Who* skit. One of the first requests

Jimmy Saville received for his show *Jim'll Fix It* was from a young viewer who wanted to meet a "real" Dalek. Naturally, Saville obliged.

Perhaps the most curious use of a Dalek was made by Katy Manning; after her stint as companion Jo Grant on *Doctor Who,* she was persuaded to do a nude photo sequence for a magazine called *Girl.* It had only the one issue, and she is seen on the cover clutching a Dalek . . . the BBC, understandably, were furious.

The Daleks have no moral virtues at all; they are completely xenophobic and kill without compunction. They are interested only in their own survival, and it's up against the wall with everyone else. They are superb scientists, without a hint of morality in their makeup. There is one thing of which you can be certain: in the fight between Good and Evil, the Daleks are always Evil incarnate. Even their mothers can't love them, for they are hatched in vast nurseries, not bred by normal reproduction. They don't (apparently) eat or sleep, and they certainly don't do anything stupid like falling in love. Their only drive is for absolute power, untainted by any other desires or emotions.

They have been compared over the years with Nazis, but this is a tenuous connection at best. Certainly there is a lack of individuality, an unquestioning obedience of orders and a willingness to die for the race—all of this epitomized the Nazi storm-trooper ideal. It isn't hard to see, though, even in the most evil member of the Nazi hierarchy, some spark of buried humanity. Even the elite had their fears and superstitions. The Daleks had none of these.

Human beings can be very good at hating other humans. Blacks, Jews, Catholics, Protestants, Arabs, and a myriad of other types all have their detractors. Within the hated minorities, hatred of the oppressors naturally grows. Racial and religious violence and bigotry can often flare, and at times it seems as though the whole human race is heading for self-destruction. Thankfully, the finer side of human nature has won so far. In the history of the human race, there have been terrible pogroms, such as the Holocaust, but there have also been many, many finer times. Few human beings have completely given themselves to the evil that lurks within. The Daleks, on the other hand, have no such restrictions; they are an unfettered race and do whatever they wish.

Perhaps this is one reason children seem drawn toward the Daleks. Children in their play often act out all of the violence, rage, and frustration that they have within. They generally do this by "living" the part of the bad guys. When playing cops and robbers, most children want to be the robbers—guns blazing, mowing down the figures of authority. So it is as Daleks that children can be the most evil things they might wish, then shuck off the trappings and return to everyday life as happy little humans again. Playing, for a while, the part of evil is a catharsis, a shedding of that evil.

Then again, maybe they just like the metallic look of the Daleks. Gleaming metal—as in toy cars, robots and suchlike—seems to have a fascination for young people. Add to that the distinctive voice, and the tendency that Daleks have to chant over and over such simple phrases as "You will obey!" or "Exterminate!" and Daleks become easy to impersonate.

Whatever the reasons for the popularity of the Daleks, that popularity cannot be denied. Over twenty-five years, the Daleks have sold millions of toys and other products. They have appeared in numerous television episodes of *Doctor Who,* and in two films of which they were the undisputed headline stars. The novel based on that original 1963 story was the first *Doctor Who* book written, and it remains in print to this day. New products are continually appearing. Public interest in the Daleks is ongoing.

This book is simply one expression

THE DALEKS

of that interest. Terry Nation is the creator of the Daleks, and their success has amazed even—perhaps especially!—him. He went almost literally overnight from being a nearly unknown writer of radio and television shows to virtually a household name. In an age when no one really paid much attention to the name on the credits of a television show, it seemed that newspapers all over England were clamoring to interview "The Dalek Man." (When Ray Cusick, the BBC designer who built the Daleks, married later that year, the papers all proclaimed: "Monster Man Marries!") The fact that he had created such popular monsters gave Terry numerous openings in which he could expand. After work on television shows like *The Avengers*, *The Saint* and *The Baron*, he created several series of his own for the BBC. Most notable of these is *Blake's Seven*, which gained a cult following in America before a single episode had even been aired.

Despite all of this, it seems that he may forever be known as The Dalek Man. When he was script-editing *The Persuaders!*, a Christmas annual based on the show was issued in England. One page contained a piece on Terry . . . and the inevitable photo accompanying the piece was of him with a Dalek.

I was one of that legion of youngsters who watched the Daleks make their first gliding steps into history in December, 1963. Over the years, I missed as few of their appearances and products as possible. Having spent the last several years earning my living mostly by writing about the history of television, the appeal of writing a book about my favorite monsters was simply too much to resist; the more so since it meant working with their creator.

What follows is a breakdown of the various appearances by the Daleks—in person or in effigy—over the past twenty-five years. Included is the original story line that Terry penned for the very first tale. From this outline, the rest of the mythos has grown. Rounding out the tale of the Daleks is a fairly complete history of the monsters. It is always subject to later additions, naturally. After all, though very little in life is certain, you may be certain that this will not exactly be the *last* word on the Daleks . . .

—John Peel, 1988

chapter 2

GROWING UP WITH THE DALEKS

BY JOHN PEEL

November 22, 1963, was a day that still lives in many memories. It was the day an assassin's bullet struck down John F. Kennedy, one of the most popular of all American presidents. The newspapers and television reports were all filled with the tale. On the same day, considerably more peacefully, C. S. Lewis died in England. He was one of the great Christian minds of the century, and had created the wonderful fantasy world of Narnia. November 22 was not a day that would be forgotten easily.

The following day, November 23, interrupted by updates on the assassination, *Doctor Who* had its first broadcast. Due to the understandable lack of interest on the part of the general population of England, the episode was even rebroadcast the following week. At that point, I was nine years old, and had just discovered science fiction. I watched the adventures of *Supercar* and *Fireball XL-5* with rapt attention. I was exactly the sort of person *Doctor Who* was aimed at. If an audience research had been conducted, it would undoubtedly have come up with a little figure that looked exactly like me. I was the target audience for *Doctor Who*. So what happened?

The first Doctor—William Hartnell—a cranky old traveler in time and space.

I missed it.

Twenty-five years later, it has become the longest-running drama series of all time. The previous record had been set by the syndicated American series *Death Valley Days*, which had run twenty-three years, from 1952–1975. Behind that lay *Gunsmoke*, a mere twenty-year veteran. (Some soap operas have, of course, run longer—but who counts them?) It's easy to see how a couple of west-

ern shows could survive so long, since westerns had dominated the TV scene since the mid-fifties with the advent of *Gunsmoke* and *The Life and Legend of Wyatt Earp* (a positive stripling, which died after a mere six years . . .). *Doctor Who,* however, is science fiction, which has *never* been very successful on TV.

The longest-running sf show on American television was *The Twilight Zone,* which lasted five years, and was constantly on the verge of cancellation. It has even returned for two years more, and another series is being filmed as I write. That's eight years in all—about one-third as long as *Doctor Who.* So why should the good Doctor still be running about the universes in his *Tardis?*

It's hard to give a good reason, and the show has been on the verge of cancellation several times. Each time, however, it bounced back and became stronger than ever.

The fifth episode of *Doctor Who* took the *Tardis* to the radiation-scarred world of Skaro, and showed us the Daleks for the first time. For me and for many fans, it was the experience of a lifetime. I hadn't seen the first four-part story of *Doctor Who.* For some reason, my family and I had decided that the show was another of those pestilential American medical shows— you know the sort. Maybe the hero

GROWING UP WITH THE DALEKS

was a neurosurgeon who had lost his memory, or something. Thus, we missed almost the whole of the first story. We finally wised up when we turned on the TV for the show following *Dr. Who*, about five minutes early. We saw four battered-looking individuals run into a police box, chased by stone-age savages. Inside, it was bigger than outside. Flicking a few controls, the police box disappeared. It reappeared on a strange planet, with a radiation-soaked dead forest.

One thing immediately became clear: if this was an American medical show, they had surgical techniques unheard of in England. Naturally enough, after that introduction, we tuned in at the correct time the next week, and saw the first adventure with the Daleks—and the rest of the following few seasons without a break. In those days, something like a fever enveloped the children of England. Later, the fans and press would dub it Dalekmania after the noted cultural phenomenon of Beatlemania. (Hey, even the Beatles appeared in a Dalek story!) Back then, though, it was just kids running about the school playgrounds, one arm straight out, one arm extended just from the elbow, yelling "Exterminate! Exterminate!" in passable renditions of the Dalek voices.

I firmly believe that one reason the Daleks were such instant successes was simply that children could impersonate them so easily. Even the worst actor in the world (and I could probably claim that distinction) could manage their odd voice, and stick his hands out. In fact, almost everyone could draw Daleks, too. There was an elegant simplicity about them that prompted kids to doodle out Daleks exterminating unpopular teachers in the margins of their notebooks. I can still pick up a pen and whip off a more than passable Dalek in less than a minute. Of course, the fact that the Daleks were homicidal maniacs did nothing to damage their popularity. Children might be so terrified of them that they would watch the show from behind items of furniture, or over their parents' shoulders, but they would watch. They wouldn't dream of not doing so. Children seem to have an instinctive rapport with homicidal maniacs—though only of the more entertaining type.

I remember going to a birthday party for a young lady friend on May 9, 1964. How can I date it so accurately? Well, the party stopped so that everyone could watch episode five of the *Doctor Who* story "The Keys of Marinus" (oddly enough, also written by Terry Nation). It seemed perfectly natural at the time. The following year, I tried very hard to get out of going to another party, because it was to be held in a church hall, and there were no televisions. Not only that, but there was a Dalek story showing at the time . . . I rushed home afterward, and my father had to tell me everything that had happened while I was away. It wasn't the same, but it was the best I could do.

There were always problems with Dalek stories back then. The next story, "The Chase," was getting to the climax when I had to go on vacation with my grandmother. On the Saturday evening, I finally managed to find, close to the camping site, a television set tuned into *Doctor Who*. The room was packed—mostly with adults—and we all watched the Daleks and the Mechonoids tear into one another. This sort of behavior wasn't limited to childhood. I was at university when "Day of the Daleks" came out, and even for the repeat showing of it, the students massed in the television room and paid attention.

Moving backward in time again, Christmas 1964 saw the sudden influx of Dalek products. My mother had wisely placed an order at the local toy store, and the gifts she ordered for me came just two days before Christmas. Thus on Christmas morning, I could read my *Dalek Annual* and play with my mystery action Dalek. This was a small replica that you put batteries in, and then set it off. It would bump into things, whirl round and charge off again, spitting sparks and noise. They were just the start of the Dalek products, a series that have continued in an almost unbroken line down to the present. They were the answer to every child's dream, and every toy store's cash register.

When I began writing, it seemed only natural that I should try penning a few Dalek stories. I used to visit a friend, Steve Evans, every Saturday, and we wrote stories, together or separately, over several years. I don't remember much about the earlier ones, but I do recall that many were Dalek adventures. Later, after discovering at the end of the seventies that there was a club for people like us, we joined the Doctor Who Appreciation Society (DWAS). It seemed inevitable that we should end up in charge of the fan fiction that was produced. Naturally enough, one or two Dalek stories were the result.

At this point, I fell in love with a young American lady who was also fond of *Doctor Who*. I sent her all kinds of presents, including Dalek bubble bath and a talking Dalek. This latter said all kinds of romantic things like: "Exterminate!" or "You will obey!" Nan must have found it at least tolerably romantic, since we've been happily married for seven years now.

GROWING UP WITH THE DALEKS

We still have both Daleks.

The appeal of the Daleks was forcibly brought home to me when I was at the DWAS Convention in 1978. One of the guests was Carole Ann Ford, the original companion from 1963. She had brought her four-year-old daughter, Tara, with her. Looking around the exhibits, Carole saw a Dalek and pointed it out to Tara. Being so young, she wasn't a viewer of *Doctor Who* on the television, and this was Tara's introduction to the monsters. At the end of the day, she asked her mother if they could take the Dalek home with them. Clearly, even on such a short association, the Dalek had considerable appeal for her.

As you can no doubt see, there has been a curious sort of inevitability about everything that has happened to me in all of this. The Daleks have always been hovering somewhere in my life. Somehow, it doesn't seem all that surprising that I should end up writing this book about those mechanical beasties, and collaborating with their creator in doing so. I would never have been able to guess it back then in December 1963, but if I had been asked what I wanted to do, it would certainly have brought the response: "Write a book about the Daleks!"

Who says childhood dreams can't come true?

CHAPTER
3

THE TELEVISION STORIES

AN EPISODE GUIDE

1. THE DALEKS

Written by	Terry Nation	Designer	Ray Cusick (except
Directed by	Christopher Barry		episode 6)
	(episodes 1, 2,		Jeremy Davis
	4, 5)	Associate Producer	Mervyn Pinfield
	Richard Martin	Producer	Verity Lambert
	(episodes 3, 6, 7)		
Production Assistant	Norman Stewart		
Assistant Floor			
Manager	Michael Ferguson	### CAST	
Costume Supervisor	Daphne Dare		
Makeup Supervisor	Elizabeth Blattner	The Doctor	William Hartnell
Theme	Ron Grainer	Ian Chesterton	William Russell
Incidental Music	Tristram Cary	Barbara Wright	Jacqueline Hill
Story Editor	David Whitaker	Susan	Carole Ann Ford

Alydon	John Lee
Ganatus	Philip Bond
Dyoni	Virginia Wetherell
Temmosus	Alan Wheatley
Elyon	Gerald Curtis
Kristas	Jonathan Crane
Antodus	Marcus Hammond
Thals	Chris Browning
	Katie Cashfield
	Vez Delahunt
	Kevin Glenny
	Ruth Harrison
	Lesley Hill
	Steve Pokol
	Jeanette Rossini
	Eric Smith
Daleks	Robert Jewell
	Kevin Manser
	Michael Summerton
	Gerald Taylor
	Peter Murphy
Dalek Voices	Peter Hawkins
	David Graham

EPISODES

1) "The Dead Planet" (12-21-63)
2) "The Survivors" (12-28-63)
3) "The Escape" (1-4-64)
4) "The Ambush" (1-11-64)
5) "The Expedition" (1-18-64)
6) "The Ordeal" (1-25-64)
7) "The Rescue" (2-1-64)

▶ **Story**

Ian Chesterton and Barbara Wright have been kidnapped by the mysterious time traveler known only as the Doctor. He claims to be trying to return them to their home in 1963, but his unpredictable *Tardis* has landed them instead in a petrified forest on the world of Skaro. The Doctor's granddaughter, Susan, finds a city of metal in the distance; the Doctor wishes to explore it. Ian won't allow him to do this, deeming it too dangerous—he is the only person able to control the *Tardis,* albeit very badly. The Doctor deliberately sabotages one of the ship's fluid links in order to provide himself with an excuse to visit the city—to refill the link with mercury.

Before they can leave the *Tardis,* there is a knock on the doors. Outside is a small box of vials, which Susan places in the ship. Later, they reach the city and split up to look for a way in. Barbara is separated from the rest and captured by the Daleks. The other three find a radiation counter inside the city, and discover that the air is lethally radioactive, explaining the weakness they feel. They also are captured by the Daleks, and Ian is paralyzed attempting to escape. The

THE TELEVISION STORIES

Daleks interrogate the Doctor and discover that the Thals have left a case of anti-radiation drugs with the travelers. They demand that one of the four fetch it, since the Daleks cannot leave the city. Susan is the only one strong enough, and their captors force her to go into the forest at night.

She recovers the drugs and meets up with the Thal who had left them— Alydon. He gives her a second set of drugs, along with his cloak. His people are looking for food, and despite the war they had with the Daleks centuries ago, they now desire peace. Susan delivers this message to the Daleks, who realize that they have a chance to trap and kill their old foes. They agree to give the Thals food, planning to kill them when they collect it. The Daleks tell the travelers, who are horrified and wish to prevent the impending massacre. The Doctor deduces that the Daleks' metal casing picks up its power from a static electricity charge in the all-metal city. Using the Thal cloak, they manage to trap one of the Daleks and kill the horrible creature inside its shell.

Ian clambers into the shell and poses as a Dalek. This enables the four heroes to escape to an elevator, where their ruse is discovered. Ian, Barbara, Susan and the Doctor escape up a tower; from there they see the Thals arriving for their food. Temmosus, the

Ian Chesterton (William Russell) becomes the first victim of the Daleks.

leader of the Thals, makes an eloquent plea to the Daleks for toleration and understanding. The travelers yell out a warning, and the Daleks exterminate Temmosus and as many others as they can. Thanks to the warning, though, most escape back to the safety of the forest, where the Daleks cannot follow. Once there, the Doctor realizes that the Daleks have his fluid link, and he must return to the city to get it. The travelers need the help of the pacifistic Thals for this, and the Doctor manages to convince them to fight in order to save their own lives.

Susan (Carole Ann Ford) and Ian (William Russell) plan their escape from the Dalek city.

Ian and Ganatus plan a rear approach to the city via a dangerous path through the Lake of Mutations. It has never been crossed safely, so the Daleks will never expect an attack from that direction. Barbara and several other Thals accompany them on this hazardous trek. Elyon is attacked and sucked into the lake, but the others reach the Drammankin Mountains and follow the Dalek water pipes into the caves leading to the city. Antodus perishes during a perilous crossing of a chasm, but the others reach the city. Meanwhile, the Doctor has used mirrors to confuse the Daleks' electronic sensors, allowing him and Alydon to lead a raiding party in through the front of the city.

The Daleks have meanwhile discovered that the Thal anti-radiation drug is lethal to them. The Daleks have become accustomed to the radiation and now need it to survive. They plan to explode another neutron bomb to make the planet uninhabitable for the Thals. As they prepare the detonation, the raiding parties discover the source of the city's power and destroy it. Without the flow of electricity, the Daleks perish. The Doctor has his fluid link, and he and his companions can leave. The Thals can now adapt the Dalek food-growing techniques and survive.

▶ Behind the Scenes

Doctor Who had been roughed out by Donald Wilson and Sydney Newman at the BBC in an attempt to find a show that the whole family could watch on early Saturday evenings.

THE TELEVISION STORIES

Newman had created another popular program for the rival ABC channel— *The Avengers*. Wilson would go on to produce one of the BBC's best money-makers, *The Forsythe Saga* (shown in the U.S. as a segment of *Masterpiece Theatre)*. Newman and Wilson wanted the new show to be entertaining and educational. The one thing Newman especially wanted to avoid was the "bug-eyed monster" that was so prevalent in American and Japanese sf films. He gave the task of creating the new show to fledgling producer Verity Lambert.

She brought in script editor David Whitaker, a man experienced in writing and in working at the BBC. Together they mapped out their plans for the new show, which would roughly combine a story set in historic times with a science-fiction adventure. The characters of Ian Chesterton and Barbara Wright would enable the audience to understand what was happening, as they were, respectively,

Susan (Carole Ann Ford) meets Alydon (John Lee), one of the gentle, beautiful Thal people.

science and history teachers. When it came to commissioning stories for the new show, Whitaker turned to his own agent and sounded out fellow writers from the agency Associated London Scripts. One of these was Terry Nation.

The idea of writing for a family show at that point was not enthralling for Terry, especially since he was then writing material steadily for stand-up comedian Tony Hancock. Hancock was at that time extremely popular in England, though he died a few years later at the peak of his career. With the steady and lucrative job for Hancock, Terry felt that he could afford to turn down David Whitaker's offer. Before he had done so, however, he and Hancock had a disagreement, leaving Terry without the commitment he had made. He then agreed to write the script Whitaker wanted, and turned in an outline for "The Survivors." Whitaker promptly accepted this and commissioned a seven-part story based upon it.

Terry sat down and whipped off the scripts, which were needed very swiftly as production came closer. Little imagining that the Daleks would be so popular, Terry simply killed them all off at the end, tying up the loose ends nicely. Then he started work on his second of three scripts for the first season ("The Keys of Marinus"). With

the completed script, Whitaker and Verity Lambert approached designer Ray Cusick for a visual concept of the Daleks. Terry had suggested that they be robotic (though *not* robots as such; they are actually cyborg creatures, using the machine to augment their weakened bodies), without normal reference features. They would possess a flexible lens, a gun and a manipulatory arm.

Cusick was (and remains) one of the BBC's best designers. With this very rough guide, plus the obvious need to have an actor inside the Dalek to move it around, he sketched out several different ideas. The budget for the show was running low, so the final design chosen was actually selected as much for the cheapness with which it could be constructed as for any other reason! The original idea for the story was that the Daleks would be controlled by a leader in a glass shell, so that the wizened Dalek creature itself could be seen within. Due to monetary shortfalls this was dropped, and all of the Daleks were constructed more or less identically.

The original intent was to construct six Dalek casings, for which Cusick was allotted the princely sum of seven hundred pounds! In the end, only four were actually constructed, one with a dilating iris in the eye stick, to be used for close-up shots. When more Daleks were needed, photo-graphic blowups were used—and you can tell! The four actors operating the Daleks found that there was some-thing appealing about the designs, and they soon entered into the spirit of the thing. They would make the Daleks be in constant slight motion, giving them an air of reality. The voices—which were metallic-sound-ing—were provided by two other ac-tors using a simple ring-modulator. It soon became apparent that since the Daleks were all identical, it was im-possible to discover which of them was supposed to be talking. Cusick added lights to their domes to enable the viewer to see that the one flashing was the one talking. The actors within the casings went along with this, and carefully learned all their lines so they could flash the lights at appropriate points. The resulting creations were both visually effective and somehow strangely appealing. Thanks to the combination of the writer's imagina-tion and the designer's skill, the Daleks had been born.*

During rehearsals, it became nec-essary to tape numbers to each of the

The Doctor (William Hartnell) meets the Daleks.

Daleks so that the director could bet-ter judge their actions. To avoid losing the tape rolls, the technicians stuck them into the Daleks' waist bands. Some publicity shots were taken at this stage, and when book illustrators saw them they assumed that the tape rolls were actually part of the cos-tumes! They accordingly drew the Daleks with little round holes behind their bands. In fact, the Daleks were never supposed to have any such ap-pendages.

Actually, they were not born quite

*For details on the creation and design of the Daleks, the reader is referred to Jeremy Bentham's excellent *Doctor Who: The Early Years* (W.H. Allen, London, 1986). This volume contains many of Ray Cusick's designs for the Daleks, and production notes on their construction and filming.

quickly enough. The first episode was supposed to have ended with Barbara being captured by a Dalek—but the Daleks had not been finished! Instead of this ending, the director used a Dalek-eye view of Barbara screaming, with just the sucker stick in view. This "what is it?" ending proved very effective, even if completely accidental. The first glimpse of the completed Dalek was seen the following week when the Doctor, Ian and Susan turned away from the radiation counter they had found, and discovered that they were surrounded by Daleks. Again, an extremely chilling moment in the story.

Ray Cusick had designed the Daleks around the shape of a salt shaker. One of his designs failed to make it into actual costume. As he explained to the *Nottinghamshire Guardian Journal* (December 23, 1964): "The bumps on the lower half of the Dalek are there because my original idea was to have lights behind them which would flash when the Dalek got too emotional. But this idea had to be abandoned as being too expensive."

The Dalek city is visually very pleasing. Cusick again went to town on the design. He had the Daleks use binary coding for their numeric system (borrowed from the world of computers), and he designed numerous Dalek symbols that were scattered throughout the city sets. Instead of rectangular doorways, arched designs were used that were sized to the Dalek machines. The human characters had to stoop to get through them, which made the whole thing more believable. Due again to budgetary restrictions, the corridors were rather short, though painted backdrops made them seem to extend further. (Actors' shadows are clearly visible on these from time to time!) For the Dalek machinery, a distinctive metallic heartbeat noise was created. This would be used in all future Dalek stories, providing a strong measure of continuity. The elevator shafts' levels were all marked in binary coding. About the city were circular designs with color-shaded areas—some form of Dalek notation system.

Since the majority of the Daleks had sucker-stick "hands," Cusick designed things to work as simply as possible for the Daleks. Controls tended to be circular, and doors were opened by passing the hand across a sensitive plate. A great deal of thought went into the design of the city.

The petrified forest was originally seen on the *Tardis* scanner at the end of an episode. Since the sets had not yet been constructed, it was a model forest. For the story involving the forest, a small set was built. Filmed from

THE TELEVISION STORIES

various angles, it looked larger than it was. Special break-off sections were constructed to allow the actors to snap the "petrified" wood, and a small model creature was made for Ian to wreck. To give the jungle a more alien look, many of the leaves were rectangular in design. The forest sounds created by the Radiophonics Department for this tale were later reused for the Doctor's return to Skaro in "Destiny of the Daleks."

The Lake of Mutations was another set. The monster that swallowed Elyon was a glass painting effect, as were the scenes of the adventurers climbing the mountain. The steps they used were eroded, as though ancient. One of the monsters seen at the lake was actually a short clip of a bizarre-looking caterpillar, taken from the BBC's stock film footage.

The final story was exciting and gripping to all but at least one person—Sidney Newman. He saw "The Daleks," and was furious. He felt that Verity Lambert had produced exactly what he didn't want—a bug-eyed-monster story. Newman called her onto the carpet, but she maintained that the Daleks were not simply monsters; they were an alien civilization. Newman remained unconvinced until the mail started pouring in. The viewers had loved the Daleks, and in fact demanded to have them return. This public tide changed Newman's complaints to praise, and after this he allowed Verity Lambert to do as she wished on the show, her excellent taste having been vindicated by the viewing public.

Though the production crew had hoped that the Daleks would go over well, no one had actually expected them to go over *this* well. No provisions had been made for their return, and one of them had been given away to a children's home! The Daleks had been killed off, but when one deals with time-and-space travel, extermination is not always as fatal as it may seem . . .

Press interest in these new monsters was aroused, and Terry suddenly discovered that he was known as the creator of the Daleks. Thanks to a good contract, he retained half of the rights to the Daleks—unusual, since the BBC does not normally allow such a division of rights. When being asked about the origin of the word *Dalek*, Terry felt that the truth was a little too prosaic—he had simply made it up—and instead told a tongue-in-cheek story that has entered Dalek mythology. To Anthony Miles of the *Daily Mirror*, he confided (December 11, 1964): "I'm very bad at making up names . . . I took Dalek from the spine of an encyclopedia. I looked up on the shelf and saw one volume marked

DAL to *LEK."* This was accepted for years, despite the fact that no encyclopedia could possibly cover such an odd spread of letters!

To illustrate the popularity of the Daleks with the viewing audience, the following were the ratings for the first story, "The Tribe of Gum" (written by Anthony Coburn) as compared with the ratings for "The Daleks":

▶ The Tribe of Gum

EPISODE #	AUDIENCE SIZE
One	9% (4.5 million)
One (repeat)	13% (6.5 million)
Two	12% (6 million)
Three	14% (7 million)
Four	13% (6.5 million)
Average for first serial:	12% (6 million)

▶ The Daleks

EPISODE #	AUDIENCE SIZE
One	14% (7 million)
Two	13% (6.5 million)
Three	18% (9 million)
Four	20% (10 million)
Five	20% (10 million)
Six	21% (10.5 million)
Seven	21% (10.5 million)
Average for second serial:	18% (9 million)

2. THE DALEK INVASION OF EARTH

Written by	Terry Nation
Directed by	Richard Martin
Fight Arranger	Peter Diamond
Production Assistant	Jane Shirley
Assistant Floor Manager	Christina Lawton
Film Cameraman	Peter Hamilton
Film Editor	John Griffiths
Lighting	Howard King
Sound	Jack Brummitt
Costume Supervisors	Daphne Dare
	Tony Pearce
Makeup Supervisor	Sonia Markham
Theme	Ron Grainer
Incidental Music	Francis Chagrin
Story Editor	David Whitaker
Designer	Spencer Chapman
Associate producer	Mervyn Pinfield
Producer	Verity Lambert

CAST

The Doctor	William Hartnell
Ian Chesterton	William Russell
Barbara Wright	Jacqueline Hill
Susan Foreman	Carole Ann Ford
Carl Tyler	Bernard Kay
David Campbell	Peter Fraser

THE TELEVISION STORIES

Dortmun	Alan Judd
Insurgent	Robert Aldous
Jenny	Ann Davies
Craddock	Michael Goldie
Thomson	Michael Davis
Baker	Richard McNeff
Larry Madison	Graham Rigby
Wells	Nicholas Smith
Slyther Operator	Nick Evans
Ashton	Patrick O'Connell
The Women in the Wood	
	Jean Conroy
	Meriel Hobson
Robomen	Martyn Huntley
	Reg Tyler
	Peter Badger
	Billy Moss
Dalek Operators	Robert Jewell
	Gerald Taylor
	Nick Evans
	Kevin Manser
	Peter Murphy
Dalek Voices	Peter Hawkins
	David Graham
The Doctor's Double	Edmund Warwick
Extras	Tony Lamden
	David Graham
	Peter Honeywell
	Roy Curtiss
	Leonard Woodrow
	Nigel Bernard
	Pat Gorman
	Peter Holmes
	Otto Friese
	Tony Poole
	John Doye
	Steve Pokol
	Patricia Phipps

Extras	Rosina Stewart
	Molly Prescott
	Susanne Charise
	Roma Milne
	Peter Diamond

EPISODES

1) "World's End" (11-21-64)
2) "The Daleks" (11-28-64)
3) "Day of Reckoning" (12-5-64)
4) "The End of Tomorrow" (12-12-64)
5) "The Waking Ally" (12-19-64)
6) "Flashpoint" (12-26-64)

▶ Story

The *Tardis* has finally brought the Doctor, Susan, Ian and Barbara back to Earth—and even to London. Yet something is terribly wrong, for the whole city is deserted and silent. Ian and the Doctor are forced to look for help when a bridge collapses, burying the *Tardis*. Instead, they discover a dead body with an odd helmet, and a flying saucer heading over the city of London. It is the year 2164 or so, and Earth has been conquered by the Daleks. Ian and the Doctor are captured as they try to rejoin the girls. Meanwhile, Susan and Barbara have been helped by Carl Tyler and David

The Daleks on Earth—or, more precisely, in the Thames.

time to free some of the captives, including the Doctor. Ian and another rebel, Larry Madison, hide out on the saucer as it takes off for the mines.

The survivors have retired in shambles. David and Susan are separated, but they eventually meet up with the injured Doctor. Tyler takes Barbara and Jenny to report back to Dortmun that the bombs were a failure. Tyler then tries to leave the city alone, though he eventually teams up with the Doctor's party. Barbara and Jenny go with Dortmun to an abandoned transport museum. There Dortmun sacrifices himself to buy the girls time to escape in a garbage truck. The Dalek saucer attacks and destroys the truck, but not before the girls have gotten to safety. They continue on to the mine, where the Doctor and the others are also headed.

Ian and Larry have arrived at the mine, which is a vast area where hundreds of prisoners work. They meet up with Wells, a supervisor trying to help the captives. Narrowly escaping death at the hands and teeth of the Slyther—a pet of the Black Dalek's—Ian and Larry end up down the mine. Larry is killed by his brother, who has been converted into a roboman. Meanwhile, Barbara and Jenny are betrayed by two women who work for the Daleks, and they too have arrived at the mines—as captives, to work for the Daleks. They

Campbell of the London resistance, and taken to their headquarters. There they meet the resistance leader, the crippled Dortmun, and Jenny, a tough-talking cynic.

The Daleks are mining in Bedfordshire, where they need extra hands. The Doctor is slated to be turned into a roboman, controlled by the sort of headpiece found on the dead man earlier. Dortmun has built bombs that he hopes will be effective against the Daleks, and the rebels stage an attack on the invaders' flying saucer. The bombs prove mostly useless, but the raid buys the rebels

THE TELEVISION STORIES

have to escape from the mines and try to stop the Daleks, so Barbara invents a fictitious uprising to get them into the control room. Spinning a complex story, she tries to distract the Daleks to give Jenny time to order the robomen to revolt. The attempt fails, and they are imprisoned to await death.

The Daleks plan to detonate a nuclear device down a fissure that stretches almost to Earth's core. This will send the molten core spinning free, and allow the Daleks to place vast motors at Earth's core, and pilot it where they will. Ian becomes accidentally locked in the bomb, but he manages to sabotage it by ripping out as many wires as he can. While the Daleks are delayed in repairing the bomb, Ian uses the opportunity to block the shaft. When the Daleks release the bomb, it is trapped near the surface instead of falling toward the center of Earth. Meanwhile, the Doctor, Susan, Tyler and David have arrived at the mines. Susan and David are sent to sabotage the Dalek power supplies, while the Doctor and Tyler invade central control.

The Daleks are preparing to leave, giving the two men the chance to slip in unobserved. They manage to free Barbara and Jenny, then order the robomen to turn on the Daleks. Unable to do anything else, the robomen obey. This begins a mass breakout of

the prisoners, who seize their chance to attack the Daleks and to flee. Ian rejoins his friends and they all vacate the mine area, heading for safety. From the hills, they watch the explosion as the mine area is turned into a seething volcano. The Dalek saucers,

Susan (Carole Ann Ford) and Barbara (Jacqueline Hill) in the ruins of London.

all gathered above the mine shaft, are sucked down and destroyed in the blast, and Earth is free once again.

The companions return to London, where the rebels help the Doctor dig out the *Tardis*. Susan and David have fallen in love, but Susan refuses to stay behind with him, thinking her grandfather needs her more. The Doctor overhears this, and deliberately locks her out of the ship. He explains to her that she's old enough to need to settle down and begin a family life with David. Convinced he is doing the right thing, the Doctor sets the *Tardis* in motion. Once it has gone, Susan and David leave to start a new life together.

▶ Behind the Scenes

The initial Dalek story had changed the thrust of *Doctor Who* entirely— and created a demand in the public to see more of the Daleks. The production crew was not slow to respond in fulfilling this desire. Though "The Dalek Invasion of Earth" (originally titled "The Return of the Daleks") was shown as the second story of the second season, it was actually filmed as the final story of the first season. It marked the departure of both Carole Ann Ford—who played Susan—and David Whitaker from his post as script editor.

There was a slight problem, of course, in that no one had expected the Daleks to be so popular when they were initially created—and they had all been killed off! Still, in a show that roams all over time and space, such matters need not be so terminal. One thing that was certain was that the second Dalek story had to be even more spectacular than the first—and what could possibly be more spectacular than having them invade Earth? If the Daleks had seemed so evil on Skaro, how much worse would they look in familiar surroundings?

The production office bravely agreed to doing an extensive amount of location shooting for the tale, to give it the proper air of authenticity. The previous tale, "The Reign of Terror," had featured the first location shooting for the series, but that was for one episode, and a relatively minor piece of it at that. For the Dalek story, a large section of the plot would be filmed in the streets of London—and in a quarry, a location that would be much overused on the program for the next twenty years or more!

The filming in London involved much-publicized photo calls at certain historic landmarks, notably Westminster Bridge. Needless to say, this raised a great deal of public interest.

THE TELEVISION STORIES

Jenny (Ann Davies) inside Dalek central. Note the circular controls, for the Daleks to operate with their sucker sticks.

On the other hand, the filming itself was done extremely early on a Sunday morning to avoid the problems of crowd control—and of trying to get permission to block off major London thoroughfares and sites! Daleks were seen moving about by the Houses of Parliament, down the Embankment area, on the Mall, around Trafalgar Square, and by the Albert Memorial in Kensington Gardens. Many of the monuments were marked with Dalek lettering, as if to reinforce the impression that the Daleks were the masters of Earth. The idea of filming so early in

the day was of great help except in one scene—in the Trafalgar Square sequence, a small vehicle can be clearly seen driving in the background!

Episodes one and three featured two extensive chase sequences filmed on these locations. The sequences were shot brilliantly for action, and accompanied by superb drumbeats on the soundtrack. The overall effect is one of sheer tension, and it has rarely been matched in films, let alone in other TV work.

The return of the Daleks had also given rise to a second problem—the production staff had not kept the original Daleks! One had been given to a children's home (it has since been recovered and restored to working order by fans of the show). Another, with a working iris, had simply vanished. As a result, fresh Daleks had to be constructed for this story. Five in all were used, one more than in the original tale, with, once again, extensive use of photographic blowups to swell the ranks! (This is especially notable in the heliport landing-area sequence.)

The Daleks for this second story were modified in a number of ways. They were all given far thicker "bumpers" on their bases. The story called for a great deal of mobility from the Daleks, and so better wheels were fitted for the operators to control them. The wheels were larger, so to cover this, the bases had to be extended. Also, a number of "fake" Daleks were constructed, so that actors could pick them up and smash them. One scene had Barbara and Jenny ram a truck through four Daleks. Clearly, breaking up four of the five Daleks would have been reckless, and these four Daleks were specially constructed break-away models. The Daleks in the first story had been unable to move off metal, so for this tale each Dalek was fitted with a dish antenna on its back. The idea was that broadcast power could be received by the Daleks. The Doctor made use of this at the end, when Susan and David severed the transmitter cables, rendering the Daleks still on the ground without power. Many of the filmed shots of the Daleks were done from either a low vantage point or a high one, allowing the Daleks to fill the screen and thus create a greater air of menace.

The first story had also given Terry and the production staff a few headaches with the problem of knowing which Dalek was in charge. For this story, two Daleks in different paint jobs were seen. The majority of them were the usual blue-and-gray coloration. The commander of the Dalek saucer had a slight difference, in that some of his vertical panels were painted red (though because of the black-and-white film, they looked black). Then, at the mine, the Dalek Supreme was also termed the Black Dalek, because his casing was entirely black. It was in fact the same casing as the saucer commander's, only with the rest of its paint job finished. Since the commander didn't turn up after the Black Dalek appeared, this was a simple matter of extra painting. On the other hand, by the end of the last episode, the black paint was beginning to flake off after being scratched!

One small difference from the first to the second story was in the tone of the Dalek voices. This time around, they were far squeakier than before. The reason for this was accidental. The BBC Radiophonics was supplying the equipment for the show to produce all special sound effects, but this equipment was then pretty new to everyone. The ring-modulator used to produce the Dalek voices was taken on location by an inexperienced sound man, and was set incorrectly. This was not noticed until after all of the location footage was shot and it was time to begin the studio work. There was simply no way that the show could afford to redub the voice or reshoot the footage, so director Richard Martin opted to change all the voices in the studio work to match that of the location filming.

The first sight of the Dalek on-

THE TELEVISION STORIES

screen was at the very end of the first episode. Ian and the Doctor back toward the river, unaware of anything amiss until they turn and see the Dalek emerging from the Thames. It's a very effective shot—and was extremely difficult to manage. The casing for the Dalek had to be dragged from the river (off-screen manipulation, naturally!) with the actor inside it. Robert Jewell, inside the Dalek, was in full scuba gear—the Thames is not a warm river. The only puzzling part of the whole thing is that we were never told exactly what the Dalek was doing in the river in the first place!

The Dalek saucer sequences were not very convincing from the model-work point of view. On the other hand, the interior sets of both the flying saucer and the mine control center were excellent. Ray Cusick's original designs for the first story were used as a basis for this tale, though the work was executed by Spencer Chapman. Despite the fact that the Daleks had invaded the whole world, only parts of England were actually seen in this tale. Various other areas, including India and Africa, were mentioned. Bedfordshire was the central area for the Dalek workings, though—conveniently for the production staff!

Though the story was ostensibly set in the future—an old calendar is dated 2164—London and its inhabitants seem very much as they were in 1964. This is partly explained as the result of the Dalek invasion. There are, however, some very nice futuristic references in the show itself. When Ian looks out of a warehouse window in the first story, a painting of the Battersea Power Station is shown, with a couple of broken chimneys. Next to it is a nuclear plant that is obviously used to supply power for the city. When the Doctor and Ian run across another captive in the Dalek saucer, he asks if they have been on one of the Moon stations, and this is why they didn't know about the invasion. Even the old woman in the wood who betrays Barbara and Jenny reminisces about better days when she visited London. She was impressed by the moving pavements and the Astronaut Fairs!

Despite all of this, the appeal of the story was that it seemed more immediate than the first Dalek tale. This was no far-flung future, but a thinly disguised here and now. The thrill was that of imagining that the Daleks might land tomorrow. The merchandising campaigns that began at this time seized on that. Many of the jigsaws featured Daleks invading Earth—and fighting quite obviously then-current soldiers and tanks. Children all over England fought their own make-believe wars with the Daleks.

The dreadful Slyther—the "horrific monster" as it actually was!

The Daleks in this story do not recognize the Doctor and his companions, though by the next story they are claimed as the Daleks' greatest foes. The Doctor conjectures—wrongly—that these are from an era before the ones he met on Skaro. The Daleks obviously communicate with central command through some form of inbuilt radio. In one case, when this is done, the Dalek raises its eye-stick. Perhaps the antenna for its radio is built into the stick? We are also told that the Dalek casing is of a special material, impervious to normal weapons. The humans call it Dalekenium.

An example of the power of suggestion that can be wielded by television is that of the Slyther. This voracious creature had been mentioned before it appeared, and regarded with dread by the inmates at the mine. It is never seen clearly on the screen, and only its claws are seen as it attacks Ashton, then Ian. Despite that, the BBC switchboard was flooded with calls from irate parents all night, complaining about the "horrific monster" that the irresponsible BBC had shown their children. In fact, the horrific monster was mostly sound effects and an actor dressed in plastic bags.

THE SPACE MUSEUM

The Daleks did not actually appear as such in this story. In the Morok museum, though, one of the exhibits is a Dalek casing, neatly labeled as being from Skaro. During a chase sequence, the Doctor hides inside it!

At the end of the story, the *Tardis* leaves Xeros. As it takes off, the picture pulls back to show two Daleks watching this. Their own time machine is ready to give chase. This was actually simply a teaser for the following week's story. For the U.S. versions of the Hartnell episodes, this ending was cut.

3. THE CHASE

Written by	Terry Nation
Directed by	Richard Martin
Fight Arranger	Peter Diamond
Production Assistants	Alan Miller
	Colin Leslie
Assistant Floor Manager	Ian Strachan
Film Cameraman	Charles Parnall
Film Editor	Norman Matthews
Lighting	Howard King
Sound	Ray Angel
Costume Supervisor	Daphne Dare
Makeup Supervisor	Sonia Markham
Incidental Music	Dudley Simpson
Story Editor	Dennis Spooner
Designers	Raymond Cusick
	John Wood
Producer	Verity Lambert

CAST

The Doctor	William Hartnell
Ian Chesterton	William Russell
Barbara Wright	Jacqueline Hill
Vicki	Maureen O'Brien
Abraham Lincoln	Robert Marsden
Francis Bacon	Roger Hammond
Queen Elizabeth I	Vivienne Bennett
William Shakespeare	Hugh Walters
Television Announcer	Richard Coe
Dalek Voices	Peter Hawkins
	David Graham
Daleks	Robert Jewell
	Kevin Manser
	Gerald Taylor
	John Scott Martin
Ian's Double	David Newman
Vicki's Double	Barbara Joss
Mire Beast	Jack Pitt
Malsan	Ian Thompson
Rynian	Hywel Bennett
Prondyn	Al Raymond
Aridian	Brian Proudfoot
Guide	Arne Gordon
Morton Dill	Peter Purves
Albert C. Richardson	Dennis Chinnery
Captain Benjamin Briggs	David Blake Kelly
Bosun	Patrick Carter
Willoughby	Douglas Ditta
Cabin Steward	Jack Pitt
Walk-Ons	Barbara Bruce
	Kathleen Heath
	Monique Lewis
	Sean Ryan
	Sally Sutherland
	Jim Tyson
	Bill Richards
	Terry Leigh
	David Pelton
	Marc Lawrence
Stuntmen	Fred Haggerty

Stuntmen	Gerry Wain
	David Connon
	Marilyn Gothard
Frankenstein	John Maxim
Dracula	Malcolm Rogers
Grey Lady	Roslyn de Winter
Robot Doctor	Edmund Warwick
Fungoids	John Scott Martin
	Jack Pitt
	Ken Tyllson
Mechonoid Voice	David Graham
Mechonoids	John Scott Martin
	Jack Pitt
	Ken Tyllson
	Murphy Grumbar
Steven Taylor	Peter Purves
Bus Conductor	Derek Ware

EPISODES

1) "The Executioners" (5-22-65)
2) "The Death of Time" (5-29-65)
3) "Flight through Eternity" (6-5-65)
4) "Journey into Terror" (6-12-65)
5) "The Death of Doctor Who" (6-19-65)
6) "The Planet of Decision" (6-26-65)

▶ Story

For once, matters are very quiet in the *Tardis,* and Vicki—Susan's replacement, a girl from Earth's future—is rather bored. The Doctor manages to fix a space-time visualizer he was given in the Space Museum, and they examine slices of Earth's history. Vicki's choice is a film clip of the Beatles—though she is surprised that they play classical music . . . the *Tardis* lands on Aridius, a desert world under twin suns. Vicki and Ian explore while the Doctor and Barbara sunbathe. The former couple get trapped underground and chased by a carnivorous mire beast. Barbara, meanwhile, sees a picture of the Daleks on the visualizer—chasing the *Tardis*. Realizing they are all in grave danger, she and the Doctor set off after Ian and Vicki, but get lost in a sandstorm. Afterward, they see that the Daleks have arrived and are searching for them.

They are saved by two Aridian natives, and taken to the Aridians' underground city. Here they are told that the mire beasts have invaded their tunnels, and the Aridians can stop them only by dynamiting the tunnels and sealing the beasts out. Ian is caught in one blast, and knocked out. Vicki goes for help but is captured by the Aridians. The Daleks have found the *Tardis* and now demand that the natives hand over the travelers—or the Daleks will destroy their city. The natives have no option, but before they can arrange the trade, the mire beasts invade their city. In the fighting, the Doctor, Barbara and Vicki flee, running into a recovered Ian. They distract the Dalek guard on the

THE TELEVISION STORIES

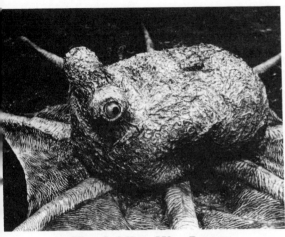

The Aridian Mire Beast.

Tardis and slip in. As the *Tardis* takes off, the furious Daleks follow in their own time machine.

The Doctor tries to lose the assassination squad, but the first place they land is on the Empire State Building, in 1965. There is no help here, so they leave, much to the amazement of Morton Dill, a wide-eyed tourist. The Daleks then land, causing Dill hysterical laughter, before going on to follow the *Tardis*. The next landing is on a sailing ship. Once again, the Doctor and his friends flee. The Daleks arrive, panicking the crew. The men jump overboard, leaving the frustrated Daleks to take off—from the now-deserted *Mary Celeste*.

The next stop is a haunted mansion. Looking for help, the Doctor and

Ian stumble upon Frankenstein's monster, while Barbara and Vicki meet Count Dracula. The Doctor believes this to be a dimension of nightmares taken from the human imagination. The Daleks arrive and instantly fall afoul of the various monsters. The fighting gives the Doctor, Ian and Barbara the chance to get to the *Tardis* and flee. It isn't until they are under way that they realize that Vicki is not aboard. She saw the *Tardis* leave and slipped into the Dalek time machine. When it takes off after the *Tardis*, she is aboard. The place they have left turns out to have been Frankenstein's House of Horrors at the 1996 World's Fair in Ghana.

The next stop is the planet Mechanus, a world overgrown with mobile vegetation. The three travelers follow a line of lights to a cave where they rest, hoping to defeat the Daleks with a bomb that the Doctor has built. The Daleks have meanwhile constructed a robot replica of the Doctor, which they send out to destroy the travelers. Vicki slips out after it and is attacked by the Fungoids. Her screams bring the Doctor and Ian to help, and she tells them about the robot. The real Doctor and the fake one engage in a duel with their walking sticks, and the Doctor rips out the robot's fuse. They retreat to the cave, where they are surrounded by Daleks. It looks like the end of the line until a hidden elevator opens and a Mechonoid invites them in.

Having no choice, the travelers follow the Mechonoid, seconds before the Daleks arrive. They are taken up to a vast city that stands above the jungle, populated entirely by the Mechonoids and one human—space pilot Steven Taylor, who has been stranded here for several years. The Mechonoids were constructed by humans who wanted to open the planet for colonization. The robots were sent here to prepare the place, but then Earth was involved in an interstellar war and the colonists never arrived. The Mechonoids want humans to look after, and will keep their captives very safe. The Daleks, meanwhile, have discovered the elevator and broken in. They invade the city to do battle with the Mechonoids and get the Doctor and his companions.

The travelers and Steven have to escape. They are 1,500 feet from the jungle floor, so they use electrical wiring to make a rope to the ground and slide to safety while the Daleks and Mechonoids clash. The Doctor's Dalek bomb explodes, setting fire to the city, which crumples behind them. Steven is lost in the collapse (though he later turns up safe in the *Tardis*). All of the Daleks are gone, and their time machine is unguarded. Ian

and Barbara realize they can use it to get home, and persuade the Doctor to set the controls for them. They get back to London in 1965 and destroy the machine to prevent the Daleks from ever using it again. The two schoolteachers now have only one real problem—how do they explain where they've been for the last two years?

▶ Behind the Scenes

This fast-paced tale introduced the Daleks' time-traveling abilities, using a sophisticated machine. Like the *Tardis,* it is dimensionally transcendental (bigger inside than out). It is so big that it even has an elevator to its second story! It travels a lot more quietly than the *Tardis,* and is fully controllable.

Once again the Daleks were slightly redesigned for this story, though they would remain constant after this tale. The bumpers around their bases were smaller again, since there was no location filming for this story. Instead of clumsy-looking antennae on their backs to receive broadcast power, the Daleks were given solar panels about their middles for power. These remained the primary source of power thereafter. Only four Dalek machines were used in this story, though the usual liberal inclusion of photographic blowups swelled their numbers. One or two of the specially constructed break-apart Daleks also featured in crowd scenes, and were systematically destroyed during the course of the episode. One Dalek, the leader, was fitted with some form of detector to trace both the *Tardis* and the time travelers. Later the same Dalek had an electrode gun instead of the tracking device, and it was used to break into the Mechonoid city.

The space-time visualizer used at the start of the story was given the Doctor in the previous tale. It was a TV screen surrounded by impressive displays, which included settings for all of the planets in the solar system. It used slotted inserts for the required scenes: Ian selected Lincoln reading the Gettysburg Address, Barbara chose Shakespeare talking with Queen Elizabeth and Sir Francis Bacon, and Vicki selected the Beatles. This was simply publicity supplied to English TV stations for the Beatles' then-latest record, "Ticket to Ride"—rather appropriate, considering all the traveling in this tale! The visualizer is seen again at the end of the story, as the Doctor and Vicki watch Ian and Barbara safely back in London. It would never appear again in the series.

A nice bit of continuity was the use of the food machine in the *Tardis*. It

had been introduced in the first Dalek tale, and had not been seen since "Beyond the Sun," the story directly after "The Daleks." Elsewhere in this story, Ian is shown reading a luridly covered book, *Monsters from Outer Space*—which he considers to be a bit far-fetched!

For the first time, we are shown the *Tardis* traveling through the space-time vortex followed by the Dalek ship. The backgrounds for these bits of model work were simply kaleidoscopic images except at the end, when a regular starscape was used.

The haunted mansion was nicely grisly. Bats on wires were used (a bit obviously). The monsters are sophisticated models along the lines of the Disney animatronics. Dracula, for example, speaks—but it is clearly a recording, as the dialogue keeps repeating in hollow tones. The Daleks cause the monsters to attack by trying to exterminate them, and thus short-circuiting them. The break-apart Daleks are extensively used here.

The Doctor's robot double was played by his stand-in, actor Edmund Warwick, with William Hartnell's voice dubbed over—sometimes rather badly. In close-up shots, Hartnell's face is mostly (though not invariably) used.

At the end of the tale, Ian and Barbara clown around at various tourist

Daleks versus Mechonoids.

spots in London. These include Trafalgar Square (also used during the Dalek invasion) and a real-life police box. To avoid the need to clear the streets during filming, these sequences were simply shot as still photographs, then played one after another.

The big showdown with the Mechonoids was perhaps the most exciting fight staged to this point on the show. The whole sequence was filmed (as opposed to videotaped, as the rest of the story was) on an unusually large set. There were only three Mechonoids built, since they were expensive and unwieldy brutes, and four Daleks. The Mechonoids

were fitted with flamethrowers, which was visually impressive. The fight sequences were filmed over and over using these seven models, then all the sequences were intercut to provide what looked like a full-scale battle, ending in the destruction of the Mechonoid city.

It was originally planned for the Mechonoids to be recurring villains for the Daleks, and indeed they were in the Dalek Christmas annuals and the comic strips. For the show, however, this proved impossible. The late Dennis Spooner was the script editor at this time, and he explained why: ''Terry put them into the script because he hoped he'd made a few quick quid [pounds] out of them, like he did with the Daleks. The designer killed it though, because they were like . . . well, the Daleks were marvelous because they didn't take up any room. In area, they didn't take up much more room than William Hartnell in a cloak. At that time we were working under very severe studio restrictions, and space-taking things *killed* it. The Mechonoids would have caught on if they'd been pushed a bit more. But they weren't pushed because no one could have stood the problems it would have caused if they had caught on! They were just physically impossible to get in and out of the studio. They were just designed wrong. Terry was very unhappy about it."

On a curious note, a record of most of the final episode and parts of the fifth was released by Century 21 Records. This firm was owned by Gerry Anderson, who was then making it very big with his own shows for the rival British network. Better known for his puppet series *Thunderbirds* and *Captain Scarlet and the Mysterons,* Anderson's companies had also founded their own weekly comic, *TV21.* The back page of this had featured Dalek stories, very successfully, and now that the firm had branched into record production, a Dalek record seemed logical. It was taken directly from the soundtracks in the BBC archives, with added narration explaining the visual aspects of the tale. In fact, two versions of the record were released. The first was withdrawn quickly, because the theme from the TV show had been used. Due to a misunderstanding, Century 21 had not realized that a separate contract was needed for permission to use it. A second version of the theme was substituted on the record from a disc that Century 21 had released earlier, and the Dalek record was rereleased. It was called simply "The Daleks" (#MA 106). Linking narration was provided by David Graham, who worked for Anderson and for *Doctor Who.*

4. MISSION TO THE UNKNOWN

Written by	Terry Nation
Directed by	Derek Martinus
Production Assistant	Angela Gordon
Assistant Floor Manager	Marjorie Yorke
Costume Supervisor	Daphne Dare
Makeup Supervisor	Sonia Markham
Story Editor	Donald Tosh
Designers	Richard Hunt
	Raymond Cusick
Producer	Verity Lambert

CAST

Marc Corey	Edward de Souza
Jeff Garvey	Barry Jackson
Gordon Lowery	Jeremy Young
Malpha	Robert Cartland
Trantis	Ronald Rich
Daleks	Robert Jewell
	Kevin Manser
	John Scott Martin
	Gerald Taylor
Dalek Voices	David Graham
	Peter Hawkins
Varga Plants	Tony Starn
	Roy Reeves
	Leslie Weeks

Planetarians	Johnny Clayton
	Pat Gorman
	Sam Mansary
	Len Russell

EPISODE

"Mission to the Unknown" (10-9-65)

▶ Story

Special Space Security (SSS) has sent a small team to the planet Kembal to investigate reports of a Dalek buildup there. Agent Marc Corey, Captain Gordon Lowery and Jeff Garvey have crash-landed there. On the surface are Varga plants, created in the laboratory by the Daleks. Their spines induce murderous frenzy in their victims, and then turn them into Varga plants themselves. This is Garvey's fate, before Corey kills him out of compassion. The Daleks know of the two humans and close in after them. They destroy the shattered ship, forcing Corey and Lowery to flee. Lowery is scratched by a Varga plant in the process.

Corey manages to spy on the Dalek city, hearing that delegates from other worlds are joining with the Daleks in an attempt to invade and conquer the Galaxy. Corey records this information for transmission back to Earth, and notices that Lowery is metamorphosing into a Varga. He is forced to kill his friend, but is in turn discovered and killed by the Daleks. His recording of their plans has fallen aside, unnoticed. The last members of the Dalek alliance now arrive on Kembal, and the Daleks are ready to begin their master plan—the destruction of Earth and the conquest of the Galaxy!

▶ Behind the Scenes

This unusual little story was actually simply a one-episode teaser for the upcoming mammoth-length "The Daleks' Masterplan." None of the usual cast was featured in this story. Since at this time, *Doctor Who* was recording almost an episode a week for a full year, it was the practice to write various regular members of the cast out of one episode from time to time to give them a break. However, this was the only episode of the series ever filmed that featured none at all of the regular cast.

This episode was actually filmed by the same crew that had just finished the previous story, "Galaxy Four," and hence is numbered as serial T/A, rather than being given a completely different number of its own ("Galaxy Four" is serial T). The episode is one of those wiped from the BBC archives, and hence no longer exists in the BBC vaults.

Special Space Security was created by Terry as a group to combat the Daleks in future stories, though they were never used again after "The Daleks' Masterplan." The SSS were planned to be a kind of elite Dalek-fighting force, and would have featured as the heroes of Terry's proposed spin-off series, *The Daleks*, had it come to fruition.

5. THE DALEKS' MASTERPLAN

Written by	Terry Nation and Dennis Spooner
Directed by	Douglas Camfield
Fight Arrangers	Derek Ware
	David Anderson
Production Assistants	Victors Ritelis
	Michael Briant
Assistant Floor Managers	Catherine Childs
	Caroline Walmsley
Costume Supervisor	Daphne Dare
Makeup Supervisor	Sonia Markham
Incidental Music	Tristram Cary
Story Editor	Donald Tosh
Designers	Raymond Cusick (episodes 1, 2, 5, 6, 7, 11)
	Barry Newbery (episodes 3, 4, 8, 9, 10)
Producer	John Wiles

CAST

The Doctor	William Hartnell
Steven	Peter Purves
Katarina	Adrienne Hill
Sara Kingdom	Jean Marsh
Bret Vyon	Nicholas Courtney
Mavic Chen	Kevin Stoney
The Meddling Monk	Peter Butterworth
Kert Gantry	Brian Cant
Lizan	Pamela Greer
Roald	Philip Anthony
Interviewer	Michael Guest
Dalek Voices	Peter Hawkins
	David Graham
Dalek Operators	Kevin Manser
	Robert Jewell
	John Scott Martin
	Gerald Taylor
Technix	Hugh Cecil
	Gary Peller
	John Cam
	David Freed
	Dennis Tate
	Ashley Bowring
Zephon	Julian Sherrier
Trantis	Roy Evans
Kirksen	Douglas Sheldon
Bors	Dallas Cavell

DOCTOR WHO AND THE DALEKS

Garge	Geoffrey Cheshire	Scott	Bruce Wightman
Criminals	Beatrice Greetz	Kephren	Jeffrey Isaac
	Jack le White	Tuthmos	Derek Ware
	Rene Heath	Hyksos	Walter Randall
	M.J. Matthews	Malpha	Bryan Mosley
Karlton	Maurice Browning	Beaus	Gerry Videl
Daxtar	Roger Avon	Old Sara	May Warden
Borkar	James Hall	Egyptians	Terry Leigh
Froyn	Bill Meilen		Valentino Musetti
Rhynmal	John Herrington		Agit Chauhan
Visian	Francis Whilley		Bruno Castagnoli
Station Sergeant	Clifford Earl		David Shaurat
First Policeman	Norman Mitchell		John Caesar
Second Policeman	Malcolm Rogers		Clay Hunter
Detective-Inspector	Kenneth Thornett		Anthony Lang
Man in Mackintosh	Reg Pritchard		Peter Johnson
Blossom LeFavre	Sheila Dunn		Len Russell
Darcy Tranton	Leonard Grahame		Ray Mironi
Steinberger P. Green	Royston Tickner		Ali Hassan
Ingmar Knopf	Mark Ross		Paul Phillips
Assistant Director	Conrad Monk		Paul Bahadur
Arab Sheik	David James		Andrew Andreas
Vamp	Paula Topham		Glenn Whitter
Clown	Robert G. Jewell	Extras	Ian East
Professor Webster	Albert Barrington		Brian Edwards
Prop Man	Buddy Windrush		Peter Holmes
Cameraman	Steve Machin		Ken MacGarvie
First Keystone Kop	Paul Sarony		John Bohea
Second Keystone			Geoffrey Witherick
Kop	Malcolm Leopold		Pat McDermott
Ingmar Knopf's			Andrea Cameron
Cameraman	Jack le White		David Anderson
Makeup Man	Harry Davies		Rocky Taylor
Cowboy	William Hall		Keith Sanderson
Saloon Bar Girl	Jean Pastell		Michael Lawrence
Chaplin	M.J. Matthews		Russell Scott
Celation	Terence Woodfield		John Daye
Gearon	Jack Pitt		Paul Sinclair
Trevor	Roger Brierley		Alan Walling
			Barry Noble

THE TELEVISION STORIES

EPISODES

▶ Story

SSS has sent a second team to Kembal, to learn the Daleks' plans. Bret Vyon and Kert Gantry are forced to crash also, and then flee for their lives as the Varga plants close in. They have overheard plans for the Daleks to take over the upcoming peace conference, and have to get away. Their aim is to warn the Guardian of the Solar System, Mavic Chen. Gantry is killed by the Daleks, but Vyon witnesses the *Tardis* landing and believes this may be his escape route. The Doctor emerges, looking for help; Steven has been wounded in the escape from the destruction of Troy, and is in danger of dying. Vyon jumps the Doctor and steals the *Tardis* key—but once inside he cannot operate the machine. Steven knocks him out, and the Doctor again looks for help as Steven sinks into a stupor. On recovering, Vyon, tied up, offers an antipoison pill to cure Steven.

The Doctor discovers the skeleton of Corey, and pockets the recording the dead agent made. Meanwhile, in the city, the members of the Dalek Alliance are gathering, representatives of various races greedy for power. The final member is none other than Mavic Chen himself. He wishes to rule far more than Earth's solar system. The Dalek Supreme watches the delegates bicker with contempt—they are all to be exterminated once their usefulness is over. Operation Inferno is about to begin. Katarina trusts Vyon now, since Steven is cured, and they all leave the *Tardis* to join with the Doctor. They then journey to the Dalek city, and the Doctor sneaks inside the conference, disguised as Zephon, one of the attendees. Now he can discover the Dalek plans.

Chen has the final item that the Daleks need—taranium, the rarest mineral in the Galaxy. It is the power source the Daleks need for their Time Destructor. Zephon sounds the alarm, and as the meeting breaks up the Doctor steals the core, with the taranium. Vyon, Steven and Katarina have meanwhile located and powered

The Daleks confer with their alien allies as they plot the Masterplan.

Mavic Chen's ship, the *Spar 7-40,* and when the Doctor arrives they take off for Earth. The Daleks manage to force the stolen ship down by remote control on the planet Desperus, a prison world, then follow it down to recover the core. Chen heads for Earth in another ship, in case somehow Vyon reaches there alive. Zephron is exterminated for having allowed this fiasco to occur. Desperus is a world where incorrigible convicts are dumped to fend for themselves or die. The arrival of the *Spar 7-40* gives hope to three prisoners—Bors, Garge and Kirksen— but the Doctor rigs a stun-charge to

the ship. Two of the men are felled, but Kirksen gets into the air lock unnoticed.

Vyon and Steven have overridden the Dalek controls and taken off again. In space, Kirksen grabs Katarina and drags her into the air lock. He demands that the ship return to Kembal, hoping for asylum and a reward from the Daleks. Vyon refuses to consider it, but Steven and the Doctor see no option. Katarina settles the problem by ejecting herself and Kirksen into space. The three men are stunned by her brave sacrifice, but can now continue on to Earth. Because of the delay, Vyon is afraid that Chen could have reached Earth first and put them on a wanted list. He lands the ship at a plant owned by Daxter, a friend—or so he thinks. Actually, Daxter has betrayed them to Karlton, Vyon's boss—who is in league with Chen. Karlton sends his best agent, Sara Kingdom, to kill the fugitives as traitors to Earth.

Sara efficiently slays Vyon, but the Doctor and Steven hide in what they think is a room. As Sara follows them in, the whole room vanishes from Earth—and reappears on the planet Mira. It was actually an experimental matter transmitter that they stumbled into. Chen contacts the Daleks to collect the core and kill the Doctor. On Mira, Sara finally listens to Steven and

THE TELEVISION STORIES

the Doctor and realizes she has been duped. Bret Vyon was her brother, and she killed him. They are forced to hide in a cave from the Visians who dwell on Mira—invisible, hostile creatures. The Daleks arrive and are attacked by the Visians. As the two forces fight, the Doctor, Steven and Sara steal the Dalek ship and take off for Earth again. In the ship is a laboratory, and the Doctor sets about making a fake core to fool the Daleks.

The Daleks manage to drag the saucer down on Kembal, and they demand the core. Steven has managed to finish the job of duplicating the core, but is in a state of shock. The Doctor agrees to turn over the core only at the *Tardis*. The Daleks, not daring to fire and chance destroying the core, must agree. The Doctor and Sarah slip into the *Tardis* with the real core, while Steven hands over the fake. The Daleks try to kill him, but fail. When Steven is inside, the Doctor sets the *Tardis* in motion.

It arrives in Liverpool, England, in 1965. The scanner is broken, so Steven and Sara have to fix it while the Doctor distracts the inquisitive local police, who are wondering where one of their telephone boxes came from. The Doctor manages to convince them only that he's a lunatic: "I am a citizen of the universe," he announces grandly. "And a gentleman

to boot." Steven, having finished the repairs, turns up disguised as a policeman from a different precinct, and takes charge of the "lunatic." The police are amazed when both enter a police box, which then vanishes . . .

The next landing is even worse—a Hollywood silent-film studio. There, rival directors want Sara and Steven for their epics, and the Doctor as a technical adviser. The Doctor proves he can achieve special effects—like making a police box vanish. Though both adventures were light-hearted for the *Tardis* crew, the Daleks have finally discovered that the Doctor gave them a fake core. They set off after the Doctor in their own time machine. Both make a stop at Lord's cricket ground—the first time ever that time machines stopped play! Then they land on the volcanic world of Tigus. Here, the Doctor hopes to fight the Daleks, but he has reckoned without the reappearance of another old foe— the Meddling Monk (from "The Time Meddler" story of the previous season). The Doctor had stranded him on Earth in A.D. 1066, but the Monk has finally escaped and wants his revenge. He puts a special lock on the *Tardis* to keep the Doctor stranded. The problem is that he can't resist boasting about it, and the Doctor figures out a way to bypass the trap.

The Monk is furious and follows

the Doctor to get his revenge. The *Tardis*—by now overheating and in need of repairs—lands in the pyramid of Cheops, as Kephren and his men are completing it. While the Doctor repairs the ship, Steven and Sara take a look around. The Daleks arrive and the companions flee—only to be captured by Kephren and his men as desecraters of the tomb. The Daleks aren't that simple to capture, and a pitched battle between them and the Egyptians erupts. The Monk, true to form, arrives in the middle of this, and mistakes the Dalek ship for the *Tardis* (he doesn't realize that the *Tardis*'s chameleon circuits don't work). Mavic Chen convinces the Daleks that the Monk might be useful to them in recovering the core.

Having overheard this, the Doctor finds the monk's *Tardis* and changes it to look like a police box. He then ambushes the Monk and puts him out of action. Sara and Steven escape from their Egyptian captors and head back to the *Tardis*. They come across a sarcophagus, which opens and a mummy emerges; it's the Monk, wrapped up for good measure by the Doctor. He tries to convince them he's on their side, but when the Daleks appear he claims to be working for them. They don't believe him and take all three captive, to trap the Doctor. The Monk now tells Sara and Steven that he was just fooling, and he's *really* on their side.

Chen demands the core in exchange for the three lives, and the Doctor is forced to comply. The exchange takes place, but before the Daleks can exterminate their foes the Egyptians attack in force. The Monk flees to his *Tardis* and takes off. However, the Doctor has stolen his directional unit, and he is stranded on a world of ice. Furious, the Monk threatens to get his revenge.

The Doctor uses the unit to steer the *Tardis* to Kembal, where the unit burns out, since it's for a different model *Tardis*. The Daleks have just arrived back with the core, and complete their Time Destructor. They imprison all of their erstwhile allies, who realize, finally, that they have been duped. Steven and Sara arrive and free them all. They vow to fight the Daleks, and they return to their home worlds. A great alliance is now building against the Daleks. The only one who doesn't cooperate is Mavic Chen, by now insane over his failures and the ultimate betrayal by the Daleks. He hands Sara and Steven over to the Daleks, who exterminate him when he demands to lead them.

The Doctor has slipped in and activates the Time Destructor, on low power, to enable him to rescue Sara and Steven. He warns them to run for

THE TELEVISION STORIES

The time meddler known only as the Monk (Peter Butterworth).

the *Tardis* and safety. Instead, Sara lingers to help him. The Time Destructor warps space and time locally, and things begin aging very rapidly—including Sara. She and the Doctor run for the *Tardis* with the machine, and the Daleks dare not fire—they might destroy the Time Destructor. On the way Sara collapses and withers to a skeleton. The Doctor also is aging, but

more slowly. Steven drags him into the safety of the *Tardis* but knocks down the Time Destructor, which then goes into reverse. The Daleks regress to metal components and embryos, which die. Kembal becomes dust and memories, the roll call of all who died to stop the Daleks' master plan.

▶ Behind the Scenes

This was the longest story ever filmed for the series, and it proved to be so great a headache that such a continuum would never be attempted again. Keeping audience interest over twelve weeks proved hard enough, even with the Daleks as the villains. It was also too much for Terry to manage alone, and he in fact wrote only episodes one to five and episode seven. The rest were penned by his friend Dennis Spooner. Spooner used the opportunity to bring back his own villain, the Meddling Monk, who had made his debut at the end of the previous season. The Monk was a popular villain, but never did return to get his revenge.

Sir Huw Weldon, then the Director General of the BBC, contacted the production office to tell them to make a monster-sized Dalek epic. The letters had been flooding in demanding more Daleks—even his own mother was a Dalek fan! In response, he felt that the *Doctor Who* team should give the public what it wanted—more and more Daleks. This order from on high wasn't exactly pleasant news to the producers, since Verity Lambert had already decided to leave the show and a whole new team was being broken in. "The Daleks' Masterplan" virtually broke them down—twelve weeks of Daleks seemed too much to make. Then, to round it all off, they were allocated an extra episode, which wound up becoming the "Mission to the Unknown" prologue to the Dalek story. Terry had his own suspicions that the BBC were trying to glut the market with Daleks and thus shut everyone up on the subject for a couple of years!

The plot was constructed so that even if viewers missed an episode, they would be able to pick up on the story line. In fact, one entire episode contained no Daleks at all—"The Feast of Steven," the only *Doctor Who* episode transmitted on Christmas Day. This was set in Liverpool, with the police wondering about the *Tardis.* It was hoped by the production team to make this as a spoof episode, with the cast from the then-popular series *Z Cars* playing themselves. The BBC hi-erarchy vetoed this idea, sadly. Still, at the end of the episode, William Hartnell stepped up to the camera, raised a glass of Christmas cheer, and wished everyone at home a happy Christmas! For years, it was rumored that Hartnell had ad-libbed this, but it had in fact been in the script for that episode. This episode was removed from the syndication packages of the story sold abroad in the sixties, so the foreign versions of the story ran only eleven episodes. (Syndicated markets in the sixties had their own special problems—for example, the story "The Crusade" was never sold to any Middle Eastern country; it was feared that since the Saracens were the villains, the Arabs would not like to watch the tale. A wise move.)

A number of people died throughout this story. Katarina had been picked up in the previous story, "The Myth Makers," but was not seen as a viable companion. Accordingly, she was killed off early in the tale in an act of heroism. She became the first of the Doctor's companions to perish. Sara Kingdom (played by Jean Marsh, best known as cocreator and star of *Upstairs, Downstairs*) also died at the end of the story. Despite this minor problem, Terry aimed to use Sara as the heroine of his proposed series *The Daleks,* to center about the SSS and its agents fighting the Daleks. Bret Vyon was played by Nicholas Courtney, to be the regular companion Brigadier Lethbridge Stewart, later, in the Jon Pertwee years.

The time-destruction sequence at the end of the story was filmed in the accepted horror-movie way. Sara's aging was done first by makeup, then by substituting an old actress. Finally, a skeleton in Sara's costume was substituted. For the effects on the Daleks, two special Daleks were built that could be caved in to look as though they were breaking down. The Dalek creatures themselves then twitched about before dying. This was the first time they had ever been shown on screen.

6. THE POWER OF THE DALEKS

Written by	David Whitaker
Directed by	Christopher Barry
Production Assistant	Michael Briant
Assistant Floor Manager	Marjorie Yorke
Assistants	Gail Paul
	Sybil Harper
	Jennifer Jones
	Lance Andrews
Grams Operator	Clive Doig
Vision Mixers	Dennis Curran

Floor Assistants	Julian Ashton
	Eddie Shah
Lighting	Graham Southcott
	Ray Hider
Sound	Buster Cole
Film Cameraman	Peter Sargent
Film Editor	Jim Latham
Costume Supervisor	Sandra Reid
Makeup Supervisor	Gillian James
Incidental Music	Tristram Cary
Story Editor	Gerry Davis
Designer	Derek Dodd
Producer	Innes Lloyd

CAST

The Doctor	Patrick Troughton
Polly	Anneke Wills
Ben	Michael Craze
The Examiner	Martin King
Quinn	Nicholas Hawtrey
Bragen	Bernard Archard
Lesterson	Robert James
Janley	Pamela Ann Davy
Hensell	Peter Bathurst
Resno	Edward Kelsey
Valmar	Richard Kane
Kebble	Steven Scott
Dalek Voices	Peter Hawkins
Daleks	Gerald Taylor
	Kevin Manser
	Robert Jewell
	John Scott Martin
Guards	Peter Forbes-Robertson
	Robert Russell

Guards   Robert Luckham
                     Tony Lammar
                     Tony Leary
                     Bernard Forest
                     Victor Munt

Rebels   Nigel Parry Jones
                     David James
                     Dave Carter
                     Philip Ryan
                     Tony Rohr
                     Nadia Baker
                     Jenny Lautrec
                     Jenny Robbins
                     Judith Pollard

EPISODES

1) 11-5-66
2) 11-12-66
3) 11-19-66
4) 11-26-66
5) 12-3-66
6) 12-10-66

▶ Story

The Doctor has regenerated, much to the disbelief of his companions, Ben and Polly. The *Tardis* lands them in A.D. 2020 on Vulcan, an Earth colony with rebel problems. An Earth examiner has arrived and is murdered in the mercury swamps. The Doctor is mistaken for the examiner by Bragen, head of security, and Quinn, the deputy governor. The Doctor plays along, avoiding the question of why he is here, naturally. Hensell, the governor, assumes it is to investigate the rebels and his handling of them. Quinn assumes it is to investigate the crashed spaceship that the scientist Lesterson

The regenerated Doctor (Patrick Troughton) in the mercury swamps of Vulcan.

THE TELEVISION STORIES

found in the swamps. Lesterson is un-cooperative, so the Doctor and his companions sneak back that night to take a look. Inside the capsule are two lifeless Daleks—and a spot where a third lay. Lesterson has taken it out. The Doctor is furious and demands that the Daleks be destroyed. Lester-son refuses.

He believes they are robots, and that if he can repower them they can be of great benefit to Vulcan. With help from Janley and Resno, he starts to power up the missing Dalek. The Doctor tries to get permission from Hensell to destroy the Daleks, but can't. When he tries to contact Earth, he discovers the apparatus sabotaged and Quinn in the room. Bragen arrests Quinn as a rebel. The Dalek, re-powered, exterminates Resno. Lester-son thinks it was an accident, and cuts the power. He removes the gun, just in case. Janley, one of the rebels, sees the possibility of using the Daleks to take over the colony. Hensell, when he finally looks at the Dalek, agrees with Lesterson that they might be useful. No one will listen to the Doc-tor.

Bragen, we learn, is secretly the rebel leader. He discredits Quinn to Hensell and is instated as assistant governor. The Dalek, by now pow-ered up again and independent, tells Lesterson that with a small amount of

The Daleks in the capsule.

equipment it can construct a meteor shield for the colony. Foolishly, Les-terson believes it and lets it try. That night, the Doctor and his companions discover that three Daleks are now working—and that they are once again armed. He still cannot convince anyone to take action, however. By now even Lesterson is getting suspi-cious of the Daleks, but Janley black-mails him to keep his fears silent. She has struck a deal with the Daleks to supply them with what they need; in return, the Daleks will help their re-bellion. The Daleks are willing to agree to anything to get the materials they want. Lesterson slips into their capsule and discovers a hidden chamber. Inside this is an assembly line with Daleks rolling off regularly—all fully armed and dangerous.

Bragen is now ready to take over the colony, and has Hensell exterminated by his Dalek "servant." But before he can kill Quinn, the Doctor, and the Doctor's companions, the Daleks—now fully prepared—cast off the guise of cooperation with the rebels and begin exterminating the humans. The foolish Janley is one of the first victims. The Doctor and Lesterson manage to reach the Dalek capsule and begin rewiring the power drainage. When the Daleks attack, Lesterson sacrifices his life so that the Doctor can finish his work. The power feed to the Daleks is reversed and they all start exploding, ending their menace. Bragen attempts to seize control again, but is killed by a disillusioned rebel. Quinn is installed as the new governor, and he begins to get the colony working again. The Doctor, Ben and Polly slip off back to the *Tardis,* and go on their way to their next adventure. Near the *Tardis,* a deactivated Dalek starts to stir again . . .

▶ Behind the Scenes

For the first time, someone other than Terry was given a Dalek story to write.

Terry had the option of first refusal on all Dalek stories, and this one he simply had to refuse. He had at the time been working as script editor on *The Baron,* and was about to take up the same post for the Linda Thorson series of *The Avengers,* and was accordingly too busy. He had an idea for a story and suggested it to the eventual scripter, his old friend David Whitaker.

Complicating the problem was the fact that William Hartnell had stepped down from the role of the Doctor—albeit somewhat reluctantly—and the new Doctor was then to be cast. Then, once David Whitaker had turned in his completed scripts, he himself left for Australia and a new series. Producer Innes Lloyd and story editor Gerry Davis were left with a script and no reviser. They called in Dennis Spooner, who had cooperated with Terry on "The Daleks' Masterplan."

"David wrote it as a straight piece for *nobody,*" Dennis explained. "You see, he knew it wasn't going to be William Hartnell, and he didn't know who it was going to be. So he wrote it as 'The Doctor,' and the Doctor was not really written at all. All the things which the Doctor said were not important. Terry had the old idea that the *plot* is what is important, so the Doctor had very little to do in the story as David wrote it. The Doctor was on the

THE TELEVISION STORIES

sidelines of the plot because Terry, like me, tried to write stories that would stand up, whether it was in *Doctor Who* or not.

"When they cast Pat Troughton, Gerry Davis didn't feel that he, as story editor, could do the amount of rewriting that was going to be involved. As story editor, you've got to liaise with makeup, costume and all the other departments; you've got to look after your producer; you've got to take the director in hand. He knew that if he took this story, he'd have to

The Doctor (Patrick Troughton), Ben (Michael Craze) and Polly (Anneke Wills) investigate the Dalek capsule.

go home for three weeks to do the amount of rewriting it needed. So he asked me to do it.

"I went in and saw Pat Troughton and I said to Pat, virtually, 'How do you see yourself as the Doctor?' That was obviously so I'd be able to write it as he wanted to play it. Basically, he saw it as Charlie Chaplin. So we went through it together, and his part expanded to just the right size. We were *enormously* overlength because David used to overwrite terribly. He wasn't a bad writer, but he was a loose writer. There was one point where he had a sequence about a food machine like you have on *Star Trek*. You dial up a meal and it comes out like raspberry ripple ice cream. It was in the original Dalek story, so it was lovely continuity, but the whole plot stopped for about ten minutes for this marvelous sequence with the food machine. I just *had* to knock it out."

The use of the Daleks to introduce Patrick Troughton to the audience was quite deliberate. This was the first time the show had attempted to change the lead actor—though it's been done a number of times successfully since then—and the BBC was not at all certain that the fans could accept it. The logical move was to wrap the story about a Dalek tale, since there would assuredly be no complaints about their return!

For this story, four new Dalek machines were built, slightly larger than the ones used during the Hartnell days. There was also a complex Dalek assembly line made for the shots inside the capsule. Dalek embryos were seen to be octopod in nature—the first time that a Dalek had actually been shown in full. (Several had been seen flopping about in "The Daleks' Masterplan," but these were the living creatures, and seen to better effect here.) As with the first story, the adult Dalek was shown as just a claw. On the assembly line, the end products were actually models available in the stores, repainted. (Models would also be used in "The Evil of the Daleks" and "Planet of the Daleks.")

7. THE EVIL OF THE DALEKS

Written by	David Whitaker
Directed by	Derek Martinus
Fight Arranger	Peter Diamond
Production Assistant	Timothy Combe
Assistant Floor Managers	David Tilley
	Margaret Rushton
Assistant	Jenny Huddleston
Grams Operator	Dave Thompson

Vision Mixers	Bruce Milliard
	John Barclay
Floor Assistants	Stephen Withers
	Graham Hoosem
Lighting	Wally Whitmore
Sound	Brian Forgham
Technical Managers	Tommy Dawson
	Neil Campbell
Costume Supervisor	Sandra Reid
Makeup Supervisor	Gillian James
Incidental Music	Dudley Simpson
Story Editors	Gerry Davis
	Peter Bryant
Designer	Chris Thompson
Producer	Innes Lloyd

CAST

The Doctor	Patrick Troughton
Jamie	Frazier Hines
Victoria Waterfield	Deborah Watling
Bob Hall	Alec Ross
Kennedy	Griffith Davies
Edward Waterfield	John Bailey
Perry	Geoffrey Colville
Mollie Dawson	Jo Robottom
Theodore Maxtible	Marius Goring
Ruth Maxtible	Brigit Forsyth
Toby	Windsor Davies
Arthur Terrall	Gary Watson
Kemel	Sonny Caldinez
Dalek Voices	Peter Hawkins
	Roy Skelton
Dalek Operators	Robert Jewell
	Gerald Taylor
	John Scott Martin
	Murphy Grumbar
	Ken Tyllsen

Driver	Len Russell
Extras	Barry Ashton
	Petal Brown
	Gillian Toll
	Tova Johannessen
	Pat Macaulay
	Judy Nicols
	Michael Brown
	Bob Wilyman
	John Hanson

EPISODES

1) 5-20-67
2) 5-27-67
3) 6-3-67
4) 6-10-67
5) 6-17-67
6) 6-24-67
7) 7-1-67

▶ Story

At the end of the previous story ("The Faceless Ones"), the Doctor and Jamie had seen someone driving off with the *Tardis*. A mechanic, Bob Hall, tells them that it was signed for by a J. Smith. Suspicious, the Doctor follows a very obvious clue to the Tricolor Coffee Shop. Perry arrives to invite him to the shop of his employer, Edward Waterfield, at ten o'clock that night. Waterfield owns an antique shop, and a man called Kennedy works for him. Kennedy sees Waterfield use a strange device to materialize an antique clock, so Kennedy returns that night to try the machine. When nothing happens, he tries to crack the safe. The machine operates, and a Dalek emerges to kill him. It then vanishes once again. The Doctor and Jamie arrive a little early for the meeting, to look about. The antiques are all genuine, yet they are also brand new, which puzzles the Doctor somewhat. Perry arrives, and together the three men find the body of Kennedy.

While Perry goes for the police, Jamie accidentally triggers a gas trap left by Waterfield. The kidnapper then drags them into his machine and they all vanish. When the Doctor recovers, he's in a country house near Canterbury in the year 1866. It is owned by Waterfield's partner, Theodore Maxtible, who introduces himself. The two men were working on time-travel experiments that resulted in the Daleks materializing. They have captured Waterfield's daughter, Victoria, and now hold her captive in the south wing of the house. With her as hostage, the two men have been forced to obey the Daleks. The Doctor confronts the Daleks, who explain that they are seeking the human factor, to transfer it to the Daleks and make them unbeatable. Jamie must attempt to rescue Victoria, and the Daleks will record his responses. The Doctor seems somewhat fascinated by the whole thing, much to Jamie's alarm.

Jamie is kidnapped by a thug called Toby, working for Arthur Terrall, Ruth Maxtible's fiancé. Terrall frees Jamie but seems oddly out of it, as if under mental control. Toby is furious that Terrall has crossed him and follows to the house, seeking revenge. There he is exterminated by the Daleks. Jamie starts the test and has to avoid death traps and face up to a huge wrestler named Kemel, who believes Jamie is a thief. Jamie tricks Kemel, but when the man falls from a window Jamie saves his life. Kemel realizes Jamie is trying to help Victoria, and he goes along with him. The Daleks are recording all of Jamie's responses. They find Victoria's room guarded by a Dalek, which they distract and throw down the stairs. Once with her, they barricade the room against the Daleks. Victoria tells them that she believes one person in the house is working willingly for the Daleks.

The Doctor and Waterfield have all the readings from Jamie that they need, which they then program into three Daleks. Waterfield, too, suspects the Doctor's scientific curiosity of getting the better of him. He hasn't known the Daleks long, but realizes they are ruthless killers, and this experiment may make them invincible. Terrall breaks into the tower room via a secret passage and kidnaps Victoria. He is being controlled by the Daleks, who also grab Kemel. Jamie escapes, back to the Doctor. The Doctor warns Ruth to evacuate the house, quickly. The three Daleks with the human factor have started playing trains, and seem most amiable. They call the Doctor Friend, and regret it when the Emperor Dalek recalls all Daleks to Skaro—where Victoria has been taken.

Maxtible was a willing agent of the Daleks, who promised him the secret of transforming iron into gold for his services. Instead, they plant a bomb in the house to destroy the machinery there, then leave. Maxtible follows them, and the Doctor, Jamie and Waterfield follow through the time tunnel seconds before the house explodes. On Skaro, they try to sneak into the Dalek city, but the Emperor has been expecting them, and they are captured as Maxtible was. Taken before the Emperor, the Doctor confronts the epitome of the Dalek—a huge, immobile creature that plots and schemes. The Doctor informs him that the humanized Daleks will cause doubt and dissent among the Daleks and this will doom the Emperor. This doesn't even worry the Emperor, for the human fac-

THE TELEVISION STORIES

tor is not what he sought—it was a smoke screen to get the Doctor to co-operate. What they were working on was the Dalek factor—a means to turn humans into Daleks. With this development, and with the *Tardis*, they can spread the Dalek factor throughout time and space. The Doctor has given them the key to final victory!

The first to fall prey to this test is Maxtible, who is transformed into a human Dalek. He hypnotizes the Doctor, who is then the second to be subjected to the treatment. Elsewhere in the city the humanized Daleks begin questioning orders—unheard-of behavior. This is reported to the Emperor, who is worried. How can they tell which Daleks are loyal and which are not? The Doctor suggests the solution—pass all the Daleks through the Dalek-Factor process. This will convert the humanized Daleks back again. The Emperor agrees and starts the operation going. The Doctor, however, is not really a Dalek—the readings taken on Jamie and Maxtible were for humans, which he certainly is not. Quickly, he reprograms the machine for the human factor.

By the time the Emperor realizes what the Doctor has done, a good proportion of the Daleks in the city have been humanized. Civil war erupts as Daleks won't obey orders, refuse to kill on command, and ask

The Emperor Dalek.

questions. The Doctor frees the human captives and they all head for the hills. Waterfield sacrifices his life to save the Doctor in the escape. Maxtible attacks the party, but Kemel grapples with him in the hills till both fall to their deaths. Watching the city, the Doctor, Jamie and Victoria see it burst into flames. The Emperor has been attacked, and the Doctor reflectively comments: "The end of the Daleks forever." They head back to the *Tardis*, hidden in the hills.

▶ Behind the Scenes

This was planned as the final Dalek story in *Doctor Who*, for the time had come when Terry was ready to market his creations in America. Having been associated with the phenomenally successful *Avengers*, he believed the time was right. To eliminate the Daleks from *Doctor Who*, this big battle story was written. After a gap of five years, when no series was made in America, the Daleks would return to the show that had spawned them.

Location filming for Maxtible's house was done at Knebworth House, once owned by Sir Arthur Sullivan (of Gilbert and Sullivan).

The Emperor Dalek was David Whitaker's idea. For many years, Terry and David had tried to work out how the Daleks were ruled, and in the comic strips for *TV21* a golden Emperor Dalek issued the orders. David took this concept and used it for

The final destruction of the Daleks—the model effects.

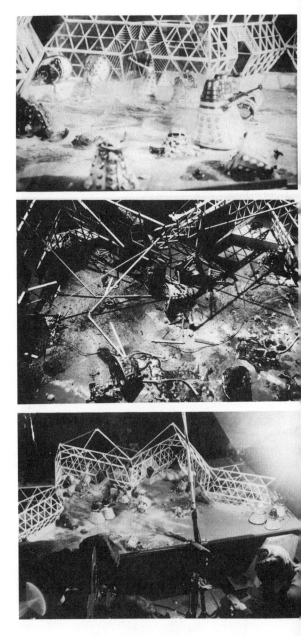

"Evil." The Emperor was actually a huge, vaguely Dalek-shaped creation. His voice (by Roy Skelton) was overlaid several times, so that it sounded as if there were many voices. It was effective but a little hard to follow. When the Doctor and Jamie were brought face to face with their ultimate foe, Jamie was supposed to remark on the size of the Dalek. Frazer, ever ready with a joke, instead pointed to the sensor spheres and said, "Look at the size of those balls . . ." (For the actual recording, he read the right line.)

The end of the Daleks involved a great deal of special-effects work. Some full-sized mock-ups were built specifically to shatter and spew colored foam all over. Others were just toy Daleks from the stores on a miniature set, exploded and filmed. The Emperor Dalek was destroyed in stages also. A miniature model of the Dalek city was used for the final battle and for the explosion into flames. The end of the Daleks, at last—for a while, at least!

The Doctor (Patrick Troughton) meets a few old "friends" at his trial—a Yeti, an Ice Warrior, a Dalek, a Cyberman and a Quark.

● THE WAR GAMES

In the final episode of the Patrick Troughton era, the Doctor had been captured and placed on trial for his life by his own people, the Time Lords.

He was accused of interfering in the events of other worlds and times, and he pleaded guilty. To explain why he did interfere, the Doctor gave a short "mind channel" demonstration of some of the evils he had combatted over the years. One of these was a Dalek (played by Robert Jewell in fresh footage for this story).

The Doctor's speech at this point is relevant: "Worst of all were the Daleks, a pitiless race of conquerors, exterminating all who came up against them. All these evils I have fought, while you have done nothing but observe."

THE MIND OF EVIL

For this Jon Pertwee story, a mind parasite creates images in the Doctor's mind of his worst fears. One of these, quite naturally, is a Dalek. The shot of the Dalek was simply a slide from "The Dalek Invasion of Earth" story.

8. DAY OF THE DALEKS

Written by	Louis Marks
Directed by	Paul Bernard
Production Assistant	Norman Stewart
Assistant Floor Manager	Sue Hedden
Assistant	Carolyn Driver
Technical Managers	Alan Horne
	Derek Martin
	Alan Arbuthnott
Sound Supervisor	Tony Millier
Grams Operator	Gordon Phillipson
Vision Mixer	Mike Catherwood
Floor Assistant	John O'Shaughnessey
Special Graphics	Sid Lomax

Fight Arranger	Rick Lester
Film Cameraman	Fred Hamilton
Film Editor	Dan Rae
Visual Effects	Jim Ward
Costumes	Mary Husband
Makeup	Heather Stewart
Masks	John Friedlander
Incidental Music	Dudley Simpson
Special Sound	Brian Hodgson
Script Editor	Terrance Dicks
Designer	David Meyerscough-Jones
Producer	Barry Letts

CAST

The Doctor	Jon Pertwee
Jo Grant	Katy Manning
Brigadier Lethbridge Stewart	Nicholas Courtney
Captain Mike Yates	Richard Franklin
Sergeant Benton	John Levene
Controller	Aubrey Woods
Anat	Anna Barry
Shura	Jimmy Winston
Boaz	Scott Fredericks
Sir Reginald Styles	Wilfred Carter
Miss Paget	Jean McFarlane
Technicians in Dalek Control	Deborah Brayshaw
	Scarlett O'Dare
	Alison Daumler
	Karen Burch
UNIT Radio Operator	Gypsie Kemp
Guerrillas	Tim Condren
	Emmett Hennessy

THE TELEVISION STORIES

Guerrillas	Stephen Ismay	Extras	Jeanne Doree
	Jim Dowdall		Iris Fry
Ogrons	Rick Lester		Beverly Grant
	Maurice Bush		Anne Priestley
	David Joyce		Jane Cousins
	Frank Menzies		Eileen Winterton
	Bruce Wells		Len Saunders
	Geoffrey Todd		Robert Bauld
Daleks	John Scott Martin		Donald Baker
	Ricky Newby		Pat Taylor
	Murphy Grumbar		Gaynor Jackson
Dalek Voices	Oliver Gilbert		Suzanne Jackson
	Peter Messaline		Terry Walsh
UNIT Guard	David Melbourne		Sue Farebrother
Daleks' Guard	Brynchan Powell		Alan Cope
UNIT Girl Operator	Bara Chambers		Sam Mansaray
UNIT Man Operator	Leon Maybanks		Michael Culling
Monia	Valentine Palmer		Harry Tierney
Manager	Peter Hill		Charles Adey-Gray
Senior Guard	Andrew Carr		Christopher Holmes
Guard at Work			Derek Hunt
Center	George Raistrick		Brian Justice
Styles' Aide	Desmond Verini		Basil Tang
Announcer	Alex MacIntosh		Vincent Wong
Extras	Michael Potter		J. Crane
	Richard Eden		M.J. Howes
	Nick Hobbs		J.H. Wright
	Stan Ross		Ron Hicks
	Terence Price		Ted Health
	Colin Richmond		Ron Collins
	Terence Brown		R. Pickford
	Hugh Rodgers		
	Keith Beresford		
	Hugh Price		
	Robin Baldwin		
	Paul Huckin		
	Pat Gorman		
	Glen Whitter		
	Betty Cameron		

EPISODES

1) 1-1-72
2) 1-8-72
3) 1-15-72
4) 1-22-72

The Doctor (Jon Pertwee) comes face to eyestick with his oldest foes.

▶ Story

We are on the brink of a third world war, and the only hope for peace seems to be a conference established by Sir Reginald Styles. When Styles claims a ghost has tried to kill him, UNIT is brought in to investigate. A wounded man is discovered with a strange gun and a device that the Doctor identifies as a portable time machine. The man is a guerrilla from the twenty-second century, and the Doctor expects further attempts to kill Styles. Anat, Shura and Boaz arrive from the future in this attempt, and mistake the Doctor for Styles. He convinces them of his identity, and the raiders need new orders. Shura attempts to get them, but is attacked by the Ogrons and wounded.

In the house, Jo accidentally triggers a time device and is whisked into the twenty-second century, where she is taken to the Controller. Realizing she is an innocent from the past, the Controller uses her trust to discover where the guerrillas he is after are located. What Jo does not discover is that Earth has been conquered by the Daleks. The guerrillas are trying to change the past and prevent the Dalek invasion. The Ogrons in the past attack Styles's house, and Anat and Shura escape to the future—taking the Doctor with them by accident. The Doctor heads for the Dalek base, intent on rescuing Jo. He is captured on his way in and interrogated by the Daleks.

The Controller saves the Doctor, hoping he can help to capture the rebels. It seems that the peace conference that Styles hosted ended in disaster—a terrible explosion killed

THE TELEVISION STORIES

all the delegates and provoked the war that it had tried to halt. History claims that Styles was a murderous fanatic who aimed to provoke the war. Afterward, humanity degenerated into bands of savages. The Daleks invaded and now run the world, raiding it for minerals. The Controller doesn't like the Daleks, but believes there is no way to defeat them. The guerrillas stage a raid to rescue the Doctor and Jo. The Doctor stops them from killing the Controller, a senseless act of revenge in his opinion.

The Doctor has realized what happened—the explosion at Styles's house was actually set off by Shura, who was trying to kill Styles. The guerrillas haven't changed history—they are responsible for what happened. The rebels realize this is true, and help the Doctor and Jo return to the twentieth century to prevent the disaster. The Ogrons corner them but the Doctor convinces the Controller that there is a chance to defeat the Daleks. He allows the Doctor to escape, and is then exterminated by the Daleks. They follow the Doctor through time to make sure that the delegates are slain and their version of history remains secure. In the past, the Doctor speaks to Shura and has the house emptied. Shura stays, and when the Daleks invade the house he blows it up, destroying them. The Doctor

knows that the future has been changed again, back to the way that it should have been—and Styles's peace conference will succeed.

▶ **Behind the Scenes**

"Day of the Daleks," the opening story of season nine, had not originally been planned as a Dalek story at all. Louis Marks's script had simply been planned as a tale in which Earth was ruled by an alien race. Producer Barry Letts and script editor Terrance Dicks wanted to start the season with a big attraction, and they decided that

The Doctor (Jon Pertwee) hides out from the Daleks.

An Ogron with his master.

the aliens should be the Daleks—always guaranteed to boost the ratings. As a result, the script was rewritten to include them. It did, however, cause a number of real problems.

The first was that the production staff didn't realize that Terry had a half-share in the Daleks, and had to be consulted whenever they were to be used. Letts and Dicks inadvertently neglected to do this, and the first they knew about the problem was when Terry's agent, Roger Hancock, called them up—having seen the first episode listed in the *Radio Times*—and told them about the agreement Terry had with the BBC. As a result, the sec-

ond episode had a voice-over crediting Terry for creating the Daleks, and the final two episodes had an on-screen credit. Terry had not written for the series since "The Daleks' Masterplan," and part of the settlement reached for the accidental breach of contract was that he be given options on writing future Dalek stories, with a guaranteed minimum of three to be used.

There was also a problem in production design, since the Daleks had not been used for three years. Only three had survived, one of which was painted gold as the leader of the Daleks. The sets built for this story were very interesting, but almost impossible for the Daleks to negotiate. As a result, the scenes set in the future were all very static when the Daleks were involved. This was less of a problem in the location shooting, thankfully.

One nice sequence is when the Daleks use a mind probe on the Doctor to confirm that he is indeed the same person they have already fought. The screen of the probe shows the title sequence pattern from the show, onto which photographs of William Hartnell and Patrick Troughton are projected.

There is a very strange mistake made when the Ogron attacks Shura. Shura puts down his gun before radio-

THE TELEVISION STORIES

ing for instructions. The Ogron then jumps Shura—who pulls his gun from its holster.

Despite whatever problems the show faced, it was, as anticipated, a tremendous success. The ratings rose as viewers tuned back in to see the return of the Daleks. Jon Pertwee was not overly happy with this, because he personally disliked the Daleks. It was obvious that they would have to return. In fact, the BBC stripped the four episodes together to produce a TV movie of the story that was repeated twice that year—also to high ratings. The Daleks showed that they still had tremendous drawing power for the audiences, and the *Radio Times* ran a competition for readers to win an actual Dalek from the show. The Daleks were also slated for promotional shows, and, obviously, for a return the following season.

The Doctor (Jon Pertwee) isn't enjoying his interrogation . . .

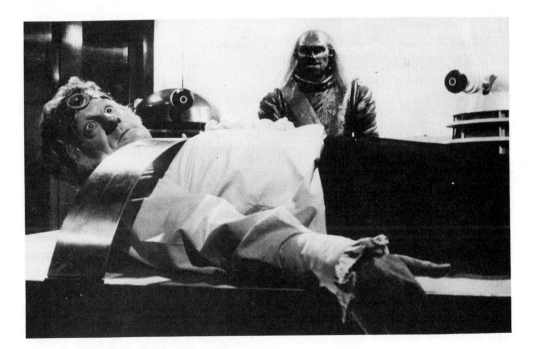

FRONTIER IN SPACE

This six-part story centered around the machinations of the Master to foment a war between Earth and the Draconian Empire. The Master was using Ogrons in his service, and this rather obviously telegraphed who the Master was really working for. The Daleks appeared for a brief scene in the final episode, as an introduction to the following story. The Daleks were hoping to begin their own wave of invasion on the Galaxy, and had hoped to weaken both the Terran and Draconian Empires by having them attack one another.

CAST

Daleks	John Scott Martin
	Cy Town
	Murphy Grumbar
Dalek Voices	Michael Wisher

9. PLANET OF THE DALEKS

Written by	Terry Nation
Directed by	David Moloney
Production Assistant	George Gallaccio
Assistant Floor Managers	Sue Hedden
	Graeme Harper
	John Cook
Assistant	Carole Bisset
Technical Managers	Derek Slee
	Ron Bristow
Sound Superviser	Tony Millier
Grams Operator	Gerry Burrowes

The Doctor (Jon Pertwee) becomes a prisoner of the Draconians.

THE TELEVISION STORIES

Vision Mixer	Michael Turner
Floor Assistant	Ken Dodds
Visual Effects	Clifford Culley
Costumes	Hazel Pethig
Makeup	Jean McMillan
Incidental Music	Dudley Simpson
Special Sound	Dick Mills
Script Editor	Terrance Dicks
Designer	John Hurst
Producer	Barry Letts

CAST

The Doctor	Jon Pertwee
Jo Grant	Katy Manning
Taron	Bernard Horsfall
Vaber	Prentiss Hancock
Codal	Tim Preece
Wester	Roy Skelton
Latep	Alan Tucker
Rebec	Jane How
Marat	Hilary Minster
Thal Pilot	Alan Casley
Spiridons	David Billa
	Ronald Gough
	Kevin Moran
	Terence Denville
	Geoff Witherick
	Kelly Varney
	Gary Dean
Dalek Voices	Roy Skelton
	Michael Wisher
Dalek Operators	John Scott Martin
	Murphy Grumbar
	Cy Town
	Tony Starr

EPISODES

1) 4-7-73
2) 4-14-73
3) 4-21-73
4) 4-28-73
5) 5-5-73
6) 5-12-73

 Story

The Doctor has had the Time Lords send the *Tardis* after the Dalek spacecraft that lifted off from the Ogron home world in the previous story. He has been wounded in the escape, though, and collapses into a healing coma before the *Tardis* arrives. Upon landing, on the planet Spiridon, Jo goes for help, which she finds in the form of three Thal soldiers: Taron, Vaber and Codal. They go to help the Doctor, and manage to get him out of the *Tardis*, which is getting covered in the strange growths of this world. Jo has become infected with a spore disease and is saved by Wester, one of the natives of this world. The Spiridons are an invisible race, and the Daleks have come here to learn their secret. With invisibility, they will be almost invincible. The Thals are here to stop them.

A second Thal ship crashes on the planet, bearing Rebec, Marat and

DOCTOR WHO AND THE DALEKS

Latep. The latest information is that there is an army of ten thousand Daleks here on Spiridon. The Daleks capture the Doctor and Codal, who are taken to the old Spiridon city for interrogation. The other Thals break in using an old cooling shaft connected to one of the planet's ice volcanoes. They join forces with the Doctor and Codal, who have escaped from their cell. The Daleks detect this, and trap them in what seems to be a huge refrigeration plant. The Doctor discovers that the Daleks have the ten thousand Daleks here in suspended animation, waiting for the perfection of invisibility so they can start their invasion of the Galaxy. Using a shaft that vents hot air, the Doctor and the Thals escape pursuit—by using a plastic sheet to catch the hot air and ride it to the surface.

The Daleks have been developing a virus that will kill all forms of life, and prepare to release it onto the planet after immunizing themselves and the Spiridons they use for slaves. Wester manages to get into the room and shatter the only vial the Daleks have. He is killed, and the Daleks with him are trapped. They cannot leave without giving the rest of their forces the deadly disease. The Doctor realizes that the only way to stop the Daleks is to entomb the frozen army permanently. This means blasting

The Doctor (Jon Pertwee) and Jo Grant (Katy Manning) find the Dalek army.

down the wall separating the city from the ice vents of the volcano.

The Dalek Supreme arrives to take personal command of the forces. The invisibility experiments are finished, so he orders the activation of the army. The Doctor and the Thals have snuck into the city and are planting their last bomb in the freezing room when the reactivation begins. They manage to place the bomb and detonate it just in time. The flood of allotropic ice engulfs the entire city, entombing the Dalek army. The Dalek Supreme is forced to abandon the city, but this is merely a setback—they can start work on digging out the army as soon as reinforcements arrive. The surviving Thals steal the Dalek Supreme's ship, to return to Skaro and their own race.

▶ Behind the Scenes

This story (originally called "Destination Daleks") was designed to take up the plot begun in "Frontier in Space," as the Doctor chased after the Daleks. For this story, four new Daleks were built to be added to the three remaining originals. One of these was the Dalek Supreme, seen in this story in rather natty gold and black. Because this creature was one of the film Daleks that had been given to Terry— and that he loaned to the series for this story only—the twin bulbs on the Dalek Supreme's dome were the squared-off type used in the film versions rather than the normal rounded bulbs. He also had an eye-stalk that flashed, thanks to the fact that instead of an iris it had a flashlight!

The scenes of the Dalek army were rather poorly animated. There was no way that the budget could afford full-sized Daleks, except in close-ups, so the Dalek army was a whole host of the commercially available toys, all repainted in the correct colors of the TV Daleks (the toy manufacturers tend to be very imaginative with the Dalek color schemes!). The problem is that they look like toy models, because they are not the correct proportions of full-sized Daleks. Added to that, they are clearly linked in small clumps and they move in these clumps. The overall effect is, sadly, unconvincing. It should be stressed that this was more the fault of the budget than of the effects team.

There was a small amount of location work for this story, as the Doctor and the Thals kill two Daleks by push-

The Doctor (Jon Pertwee) disposing of a Dalek in a pool of allotropic ice.

ing them into an ice pool. The effects team used ramps for the Daleks to be pushed down, and carefully filmed angles obscured this fact—a detail the location photographer overlooked when taking publicity stills!

On a personal note, the Thal heroine Rebec was named after Terry's daughter Rebecca. She was at this time the perfect age to enjoy this, and had also been the eponymous heroine of the novel *Rebecca's World* that Terry had written.

10. DEATH TO THE DALEKS

Written by	Terry Nation
Directed by	Michael Briant
Production Assistant	Chris D'Oyly-John
Assistant Floor Manager	Richard Leyland
Director's Assistant	Margaret Lewty
Technical Managers	Derek Slee
	Eric Wallis
Sound Supervisor	Richard Chubb
Grams Operator	Gordon Phillipson
Vision Mixer	Nick Lake
Floor Assistant	Malcolm Hamilton
Film Cameraman	Bill Matthews
Assistant Film Cameramen	Martin Patmore
	Ian Pugsley

Film Sound	Bill Chesneau
Assistant Film Sound Recordists	Chris Lovelock
	Clive Derbyshire
Grip	Alan Wood
Film Lighting	Dave Smith
Film Editors	Bob Rymer
	Larry Toft
Visual Effects	Jim Ward
	Mat Irvine
Masks	John Friedlander
Fight Arranger	Terry Walsh
Costumes	L. Rowland Warne
Makeup	Magdalen Gaffney
	Cynthia Goodwin
Incidental Music	Carey Blyton
Performed by	The London Saxophone Quartet
Special Sound	Dick Mills
Script Editors	Terrance Dicks
	Robert Holmes
Designer	Colin Green
Producer	Barry Letts

CAST

The Doctor	Jon Pertwee
Sarah Jane Smith	Elisabeth Sladen
Lieutenant Dan Galloway	Duncan Lamont
Lieutenant Peter Hamilton	Julian Fox
Jill Tarrant	Joy Harrison
Commander Stewart	Noel Seiler
Captain Richard Railton	John Abineri
Bellal	Arnold Yarrow
High Priest	Mostyn Evans

THE TELEVISION STORIES

Gotal	Roy Heyman	Extras	Roy Pearce
Zombies	Steven Ismay		Terry Denville
	Terry Walsh		Nigel Wynder
Dalek Voices	Michael Wisher		Max Faulkner
Dalek Operators	John Scott Martin		Tex Fuller
	Cy Town	Stuntmen	Terry Walsh
	Murphy Grumbar		Alan Chuntz
Exxilons	David Rolfe		Marc Boyle
	Mike Reynal		
	Derek Shafer		
	Terry Sartain		
	Kevin Moran		
	Leslie Bates		
	Dennis Plenty		
	Steven Ismaym		
	Bob Blaine		

EPISODES

1) 2-23-74
2) 3-2-74
3) 3-9-74
4) 3-16-74

The Daleks find that they cannot exterminate the Doctor (Jon Pertwee).

▶ Story

A space plague is sweeping across the Galaxy, and there is only one cure—the mineral Parrinium. It is discovered only on Exxilon, a strange, hidden planet. An Earth ship heads there, led by Commander Stewart. The ship is drained of power and crashes close to a fabulous crystalline city. The power drain is extremely pervasive; it affects even the *Tardis,* dragging it down to Exxilon and stranding it there. The Doctor and Sarah set out, and get separated in the mists. The Doctor runs into the survivors of the crash—Stewart is injured, and Galloway, Hamilton, Jill Tarrant, and Railton also remain alive. Sarah is captured by the native Exxilons and sentenced to death for having gazed on their holy city.

THE TELEVISION STORIES

The city was created by the Exxilon race centuries earlier. It rejected them as being too primitive, and forced them out. The Exxilons mostly returned to savagery, though some retained a little dignity and civilized ways. The city was self-sustaining, draining power from any source, and is the cause of the power drainages. It has tendrils that burrow into the ground, seeking metals to replace damaged parts. It can go on forever . . .

Another ship lands, this time containing Daleks. The power drain has forced them down—and robbed their weapons of effectiveness. The Daleks almost panic when they are powerless. Railton offers an alliance when the Daleks claim to be here for the Parrinium also, saying that their race also has been affected. They are lying, though. They are not troubled by the plague, but they know that if they have the only antidote they can enslave many worlds. While the Daleks on the ground go with the humans, other Daleks in the ship modify their ray guns and replace them with machine guns; they are armed once again.

The native Exxilons have by now captured the humans and the initial Dalek patrol, planning to sacrifice them all. The Doctor manages to rescue Sarah temporarily, and when the armed Daleks arrive and begin killing the natives, he and Sarah slip further into the tunnels under the city. The Daleks soon take command of the natives and the living humans. All are set to work mining the Parrinium and loading the stuff into the Dalek ship. The Doctor and Sarah manage to evade a pursuing Dalek, which is destroyed by one of the questing tendrils from the city. They are then found and helped by Bellal, one of the civilized natives. He tells them about the city, and the Doctor realizes that the only way they can escape from this planet is if he can somehow destroy the computer that runs the city. The Daleks have meanwhile come to the same conclusion. They send two Daleks to attempt entry through the tunnels the Doctor has taken. They also send Galloway and Hamilton up the outside of the city, to plant bombs to destroy the collecting antenna.

The way into the city is guarded by traps controlled by the computer. The Doctor and Bellal manage to thread their way through them to the computer room, where the Doctor proceeds to reprogram the machine. The computer, aware that it is in trouble, begins creating two zombies to attack and destroy the invaders. The two Daleks, using their inbuilt computers, also figure out the path through the deadly maze, and arrive as the zombies emerge. Realizing that the Daleks

The Exxilons.

are the more dangerous, the zombies attack them, giving the Doctor and Bellal a chance to escape. The Daleks are destroyed, but the computer is beginning to collapse.

Galloway and Hamilton destroy the collecting antenna, but save one bomb. Galloway manages to slip aboard the Dalek ship with it. The Daleks have finished loading the mineral, and now aim to go into orbit and release a plague bomb to make the planet unapproachable. They can then begin their blackmail of the rest of the Galaxy. As the ship takes off, however, Galloway detonates the stolen bomb. The ship is destroyed. Sarah and Jill now reveal that the Parrinium is actually on the Earth ship—

they loaded nothing but sand into the Dalek saucer. The humans take off with the antidote for the plague. The Doctor and Sarah can leave whenever they like, and watch as the Exxilon city melts into nothingness now that the computer has been destroyed.

▶ **Behind the Scenes**

For this story, the three working Daleks still available at the BBC were restored to their silver look. The set designs in the Dalek saucer were based on the older stories, giving it a fine air of uniformity once more. The Daleks were also seen using their brains, both in figuring out the path to the computer and in improvising working weapons for themselves.

There is one piece of bad editing at the end of the first episode. The show was supposed to end with the Daleks intending to exterminate the humans, then pick up in episode two with their guns not working. Instead, it is obvious at the end of the first part that the Dalek guns aren't working, somewhat ruining the cliff-hanger.

The initial title for this story was to be ''The Exxilons,'' after the native species. These were silicon-based life-forms (hence their immunity to the plague threatening the Galaxy). Incoming script editor Robert Holmes reputedly retitled the story because he hated the Daleks—and "Death to the Daleks" reflected his own feelings!

This story has recently been issued on videotape in England, and the release was celebrated at Virgin Records in London on August 6, 1987. Jon Pertwee signed copies, cutout Daleks were in evidence, and a number of monsters from the show came along—fans wearing official costumes from the BBC exhibitions.

11. GENESIS OF THE DALEKS

Written by	Terry Nation
Directed by	David Moloney
Production Unit Manager	George Gallaccio
Production Assistant	Rosemary Crowson
Visual Effects Designer	Peter Day
Davros's Mask Designer	John Friedlander
Costume Designer	Barbara Kidd
Makeup Supervisor	Sylvia James
Lighting	Duncan Brown
Studio Sound	Tony Millier
Designer	David Spode
Special Sound	Dick Mills
Title Sequence	Bernard Lodge
Theme	Ron Grainer
Incidental Music	Dudley Simpson
Script Editor	Robert Holmes
Producer	Philip Hinchcliffe

CAST

The Doctor	Tom Baker
Sarah Jane Smith	Elizabeth Sladen
Harry Sullivan	Ian Marter
Davros	Michael Wisher
Nyder	Peter Miles
Gharman	Dennis Chinnery
Ravon	Guy Siner
Time Lord	John Franklyn-Robbins
Sevrin	Stephen Yardley
Ronson	James Garbutt
Tane	Drew Wood
Gerrill	Jeremy Chandler
Kaled Leader	Richard Reeves
Thal Soldiers	Pat Gorman
	Hilary Minster
	John Gleeson
Kowell	Tom Georgeson
Mogran	Ivor Roberts
Thal Politician	Michael Lynch
Thal Guard	Max Faulkner
Bettan	Harriet Philpin
Kaled Guard	Peter Mantle
Kravos	Andrew Johns
Daleks	John Scott Martin
	Cy Town
	Keith Ashley
Dalek Voice	Roy Skelton

EPISODES

 Story

The Time Lords have foreseen a time when the Daleks will destroy all other life-forms and dominate the universe. They ask the Doctor to go back to the Daleks' origin and either destroy the Daleks or ensure that they evolve into a less-aggressive species. The Doctor, despite his reluctance to act again as an agent for the Time Lords, agrees to try this. He, Harry and Sarah then find themselves on Skaro during the Thousand Year War between the Kaleds and the Thals. The Doctor and Harry are captured by the Kaleds and taken for interrogation. Sarah, stunned in an attack, wanders the battlefield and is chased by the Mutos—genetic mutations loathed by both sides. She manages to evade them for a while, and arrives at a test site in time to see Davros, the brilliant Kaled scientist, and his associate Gharman testing a new machine—the Dalek. Davros is testing its ability to kill.

Sarah is captured by the Mutos but saved by one of their number, Sevrin, when the rest want to kill her. She and Sevrin are captured by a Thal patrol and taken to work for them. They have a missile filled with radioactive material that they aim to launch at the Kaled dome. The slaves are to load it, until they die from radiation poisoning. Meanwhile, in the Kaled city, the Doctor and Harry are taken to one of the senior scientists, Ronson. He is reluctant at first to believe they are aliens, and takes their possessions, including the time ring that they need to return to the *Tardis* when they have finished their mission. Davros arrives with his Dalek, to announce it to the staff. Realizing he is an alien, the Dalek tries to kill the Doctor. Ronson stops it, to Davros's fury. Ronson wants to interrogate the prisoners, which Davros agrees to. The Dalek can kill them later.

Ronson and some of his colleagues are disturbed by Davros's Daleks. He explains to the Doctor that Davros has programmed all mercy and compassion from them, and warped their genetic development. The Doctor volunteers to carry a message to the Kaled rulers to alert them to this danger, and Ronson helps them to escape from the bunker to the above-ground city. There, the Doctor and Harry contact the rulers, who agree to force

THE TELEVISION STORIES

Davros to halt his work while they investigate the allegations made against him. Davros agrees to this, planning treachery all along—he dares not let the rulers see what he is doing. The Doctor discovers that Sarah is in the Thal dome, so he and Harry make their way over there. To their surprise, Davros and his assistant Nyder are also there.

Davros betrays the Kaleds to the Thals, to stop the Kaleds' interference in his experiments. The dome over the Kaled city is impregnable, but Davros gives the Thals a chemical formula that will erode the dome and allow their missile to destroy the city. Davros claims he only wants an end to the war. The Thals instantly begin the countdown for their rocket, while

Tom Baker poses with Daleks outside the BBC Television Centre.

Davros (Michael Wisher) and his Daleks.

Harry and the Doctor rescue Sarah and the other prisoners. While his friends lead the escape from the Thal city, the Doctor tries to sabotage the rocket. He fails and is captured. The rocket launches, and totally annihilates the Kaled race. The Thals rejoice at what they believe is their victory, and free all prisoners, including the Doctor. The only one who will listen to the Doctor's warnings of Davros's treachery is a soldier called Bettan.

She and he see the arrival of the first Dalek forces, which start exterminating the Thals.

In the bunker, Gharman has begun to worry about Davros's increasing insanity. He and some of the other scientists try to raise support to stop Davros, but Gharman is betrayed by Nyder and captured by Davros. The Doctor and Bettan meet up with Sarah, Harry and Sevran in the wilderness. Bettan and Sevran agree to round up what survivors they can find for an attack to seal the Daleks in the bunker. The Doctor, Harry and Sarah head back there to try to recover the time ring. As they enter, they are captured by Davros and Nyder. Threatening to torture Sarah and Harry, Davros forces the Doctor to recount what he knows of the Daleks' failures over the next few millennia. Davros records this information, planning to program it into the Dalek memory banks so that they will not fail.

Gharman and his friends manage to start their rebellion, and they demand that Davros stop production of the Daleks. Davros pretends to agree, but actually recalls his operating Daleks. They then surround and exterminate the "traitors." The Doctor, Sarah and Harry have been freed and manage to capture Nyder, forcing him to give them the time ring and the tape of the Daleks' weaknesses, which the

Doctor then destroys. He and his friends escape from the bunker just seconds before Bettan and her makeshift troops seal it up—for perhaps a thousand years. On a monitor, they all see the end of the witch-hunt below. With the "traitors" dead, Davros discovers that he has lost control of the Daleks. They have begun their production lineup, and kill all the remaining Kaleds. When Davros tries to stop them, they exterminate him. The Daleks know that they must wait, but they will some day be ready to break out and conquer the universe.

▶ Behind the Scenes

For the first time, we get a more complete account of the creation of the Daleks. Terry felt that the time was right to investigate just how the Daleks had come about in the first place— something rather skimmed over in "The Daleks" itself. Accordingly, he came up with the idea of the Thousand Year War and the character of Davros, their creator.

Davros came into being for two reasons. Firstly, the Daleks tend to talk in a slow monotone, and Terry realized that this was boring for long speeches. What he needed was a spokesman for the Daleks who could be a trifle more human, with a voice that was easier to listen to. Secondly, Terry wanted someone who was a sort of cross between human and Dalek, and Davros was at that half-way stage. The Daleks could then become the "children" that he could not physically have.

To create Davros, the designer based his chair on the Dalek form. Actor Michael Wisher then had to sit for a makeup mask to be fashioned from his face and then uglified by monster-maker John Friedlander. This was fitted to his face in several sections— some of the publicity stills show him minus the awkward mouth-piece, which was omitted for the rehearsals. This mask was reused for the future actors who played the part of Davros, despite the fact that it was custom-tailored to Wisher's face. As a result it looks definitely unconvincing after this tale. For this story, however, it was most impressive.

The deteriorating condition of the Daleks themselves left only three of the costumes fit for use. Camera trickery and reshot angles made them look like an army, but no more than three were ever seen at one time.

This story was steeped in violence, one of the trademarks of the Hincliffe-Holmes era of the show. It garnered much criticism at the time for this, notably from the press and the public watchdogs. They complained of the slow-motion machine-gunning shown in the first episode in the Kaled-Thal fighting, and of the fact that the Doctor and his companions have to rob corpses to get themselves gas masks. In fact, the whole program is pretty violent—but considering that it is about warfare, it would be hard-pressed to be anything else. Unlike many later stories, the violence that is shown is at least integral to the tale, and not spurious.

The fans also complained loudly, for a different reason. In the course of "The Daleks" story in 1963, a totally different account of their origin had been presented—one that was contradicted (at least apparently) here. The fans, not unnaturally, were pretty annoyed by this, and matters were not helped when Terry was misquoted by the press as fobbing off their complaints with: "History is always being rewritten." What he actually meant was that history is always being discovered to be slightly different. The earlier story was true as far as it went; "Genesis of the Daleks" merely presented a case of more information being discovered during the intervening years. It was meant to expand on the original tale, not to flatly contradict it.

Davros would return in "Destiny of the Daleks," despite his apparent death in this story. In fact, Terry had written into his script for "Genesis" that the camera should show that Davros's life-support light was still on after he was "exterminated." The concept was that he would be in a coma for years, which the Daleks would later discover from their records. Sadly, the editing of this story cut the required close-up, and the intention was missed.

Michael Wisher had a fun time playing Davros, and like most actors clowned around a lot during rehearsals. Someone wondered how Davros managed to go to the bathroom if he was confined to his chair, so Wisher whipped about in his chair and dribbled water behind him as he went.

Despite the criticism from the fans (who on the whole enjoyed the tale despite the origin quibbles) and the critics who hated the violence, this tale proved to be an extremely popular one. It was repeated (not a normal practice with the BBC) and again garnered good ratings. Besides the Daleks, the character of Davros caught the public eye. A record based on this story was also issued, though naturally the tale was somewhat condensed to fill only thirty minutes (BBC Records REH 364).

12. DESTINY OF THE DALEKS

Written by	Terry Nation
Directed by	Ken Grieve
Incidental Music	Dudley Simpson
Special Sound	Dick Mills
Production Assistant	Henry Foster
Production Unit Manager	John Nathan-Turner
Director's Assistant	Roz Berrystone

The Doctor (Tom Baker) and Romana (Lalla Ward) with the Daleks.

Assistant Floor Manager	David Tilley
Film Cameramen	Phil Law
	Kevin Rowley
Steadycam	Fred Hamilton
Film Recordist	Graham Bedwell
Film Editor	Dick Allen
Studio Lighting	John Dixon
Studio Sound	Clive Gifford
Technical Manager	John Dean
Senior Cameraman	Alec Wheal
Visual Effects Designer	Peter Logan
Electronics Effects	Dave Jervis
Vision Mixer	Nigel Finnis
Videotape Editor	Alan Goddard
Costume Designer	June Hudson
Makeup Artist	Cecile Hay-Arthur
Script Editor	Douglas Adams
Designer	Ken Ledsham
Producer	Graham Williams

CAST

The Doctor	Tom Baker
Romana	Lalla Ward
Tysson	Tim Barlow
Commander Sharrel	Peter Straker
Davros	David Gooderson
Agella	Suzanne Danielle
Lan	Tony Osoba
Movellan Guard	Cassandra
Jall	Penny Casdagli
Veldan	David Yip
Dalek Operators	Cy Town
	Mike Mungarvan
Dalek Voices	Roy Skelton

EPISODES

1) 9-1-79
2) 9-8-79
3) 9-15-79
4) 9-22-79

▶ Story

Romana has just regenerated, and K9 has mechanical laryngitis as the *Tardis* lands. The planet has a strange familiarity about it for the Doctor, and he and Romana can feel drilling operations going on below their feet. They see a group of ragged individuals burying someone. As the Doctor and Romana discover that the body died of malnutrition and exhaustion, a space-ship lands. Before they can investigate, they are forced undercover by a series of explosions. The Doctor is trapped, and Romana heads for help. The Doctor is rescued by three tall, beautiful Movellans and taken to their ship, which has just landed. Romana returns for the Doctor, but finds him missing. Tysson appears, and, startled, Romana falls down a shaft. When she recovers, she is captured by the Daleks.

The Doctor learns that this is Skaro, and the Movellans are here to stop the Daleks in whatever they are doing. The Movellans capture Tysson, who explains that he is an escaped prisoner, and that Romana has been captured. The Doctor wants to get into the city, and Sharrel, the commander, agrees. Lan and Agella will go with them all. Romana is meanwhile judged by the Daleks to be no threat, and is placed in a work group. To escape, she stops her hearts and feigns death so she'll be tossed outside as useless. The Doctor meanwhile discovers that this is the site of the old Dalek city above the bunkers he visited previously. The Daleks are looking for something in the lower levels, using incomplete maps. The Doctor knows a quicker way down, and they retreat. Lan is killed as they do so, but they meet up with Romana.

In the lower level, they discover what the Doctor had feared—Davros. He comes back to life as they hear the Daleks approaching. Agella is killed in the falling rubble as they escape, taking Davros as hostage. Trapped, the Doctor stalls for time while the others go back to the Movellans for help. The Doctor is found, but he has booby-trapped Davros's chair and threatens to kill him unless the Daleks release their prisoners and give him time to escape. Knowing he is serious, Davros makes the Daleks agree. When the Doctor gets away, he meets up with Tysson, who has organized the other prisoners into a fighting force. Romana, back at the Movellan craft, sees Lan and Agella, both perfectly well. Sharrel has her captured to bring the Doctor out. They plan to use him, and then destroy the planet with a nova bomb.

The Doctor has deduced that the Movellans are robots designed to look humanoid, and powered by small packs at their belts that can be rewired. He is captured by the Movellans and discovers that they are doing battle with the Daleks for the suprem-

Romana (Lalla Ward) comes face to eyestick with a Dalek.

acy of the Galaxy. The two fleets are evenly matched, and both use computers to determine strategy. Neither side can start a war without the certainty of winning. This is what the Daleks need Davros for, and now the Movellans want the Doctor. Tyssan starts to capture Movellan guards and reprogram them to help in an assault on their ship. Davros, meanwhile, worried about the Movellans using the Doctor, readies all but one Dalek as living bombs to destroy the Movellans.

Tyssan's raid on the ship succeeds, and the ex-prisoners now have a means of getting home again. The Doctor sets out for the bunker to stop Davros, and Romana heads after Sharrel, who wants to set off the nova bomb. She defeats him and defuses the bomb. The Doctor disposes of the final Dalek with Davros, and then detonates the Dalek suicide squad before it can reach the ship. Davros is put into cryogenic suspension, to be taken back to Earth and be tried for his crimes against all sentient beings.

▶ Behind the Scenes

This sequel to "Genesis of the Daleks" was perhaps one of the most troubled Dalek stories ever filmed. Terry's original script was much rewritten by Douglas Adams, who interjected a great number of silly jokes. Adams—author of the immensely popular *Hitch-Hiker's Guide to the Galaxy* books—had no prior experience at script editing, and simply wrote in many silly lines, often referring back to his own stories. For example, when the Doctor is trapped, he is seen reading a book called *Origin of the Universe* by Oolon Colluphid—a character from *Hitch-Hiker*.

In addition, the original Romana, Mary Tamm, had left the show (as she had told Graham Williams she would from the beginning) and no new companion had been selected. Since most of the scripts for the season had been written by this time, the obvious move of regenerating Romana was opted for. A hastily written regeneration scene was thus tacked onto the beginning of the story by Douglas Adams—played almost entirely for laughs.

Since Davros had proven to be very popular in "Genesis," the production team wanted him back again. The trouble was that Michael Wisher, who had originally played the part, was in Australia at the time. So the role was recast for David Gooderson. The old costume and mask originally made for Wisher was used for him—and it was not a good fit. Added to that, his voice was not modulated as

Wisher's had been, and he sounds totally wrong.

Finally, when it came time for the Daleks to be brought out of mothballs for this tale, it was discovered that only five were in working shape, and those were all pretty badly off, not having been stored properly. All had broken slats, chipped paint, and their tops would not stay in one place. To cope with this, the effects men simply drilled holes in their lids and inserted doweled sticks to keep the lids on—and left the ends of the dowels protruding! They looked like the press-the-button-and-make-them-speak models available in the shops. Not only that, but the Daleks were not even given a new coat of paint, and they look positively terrible on-screen.

Compounding this, no money was spent in constructing the usual lightweight Daleks for the explosion sequences—so the real Daleks were used! When this story was over, none of the Dalek machines were in any shape to ever be used again.

On the bright side of this story, the Movellans were realized extremely well, and the model effects of their ship landing and burrowing into the sand are probably the best done in the show to this point. The sets in the Dalek city were very nice, and the interior of the Movellan ship was also a delight to the eye. The Daleks are seen at one point using infrared to track the escaped Doctor, which was a first for the show and extremely logical for the Daleks. On the other hand, the rewritten script calls the Daleks "robots" throughout, and claims that they were once organic beings, as though they had somehow mutated into purely robotic creatures. This is a completely untrue impression, sadly. The Daleks were always cyborgs—half organic, augmented by their travel machines and inbuilt computer and weaponry systems.

THE FIVE DOCTORS

For the twentieth anniversary of the show, a special story was written containing all of the previous Doctors (albeit Tom Baker only in a clip from the unfinished story ("Shada"), and many of the companions. Also featured were a selection of old monsters, including, naturally, a Dalek.

This was seen hunting the first Doctor (played here by Richard Hurndall, since William Hartnell had died in 1975) and Susan (played by Carole Ann Ford). It soon destroyed itself, by reflecting its own destructive ray into a mirror.

CAST

Dalek Voice	Roy Skelton
Dalek Operator	John Scott Martin

(Transmitted 11-25-83)

13. RESURRECTION OF THE DALEKS

Written by	Eric Saward
Directed by	Matthew Robinson
Incidental Music	Malcolm Clarke
Special Sound	Dick Mills
Production Manager	Corinne Hollingworth
Production Associate	June Collins
Production Assistant	Joy Sinclair
Assistant Floor Manager	Matthew Burge
Film Cameraman	Ian Punter
Film Sound	Bob Roberts
Film Editor	Dan Rae
Visual Effects Designer	Peter Wragg
Video Effects	Dave Chapman
Vision Mixer	Paul Wheeler
Technical Coordinator	Alan Arbuthnott
Camera Supervisor	Alec Wheal
Videotape Editor	Hugh Parson
Lighting Director	Ron Bristow
Studio Sound	Scott Talbott
Costume Designer	Janet Tharby

Makeup Designer	Eileen Mair
Script Editor	Eric Saward
Title Sequence	Sid Sutton
Designer	John Anderson
Producer	John Nathan-Turner

CAST

The Doctor	Peter Davison
Tegan Jovanka	Janet Fielding
Turlough	Mark Strickson
Stien	Rodney Bewes
Styles	Rula Lenska
Colonel Archer	Del Henney
Lytton	Maurice Colbourne
Professor Laird	Chloe Ashcroft
Sergeant Calder	Philip McGough
Davros	Terry Malloy
Mercer	Jim Findley
Kiston	Les Grantham
Osborn	Sneh Gupta
Trooper	Roger Davenport
Crewmembers	John Adam Baker
	Linsey Turner
Galloway	William Sleigh
Dalek Voices	Brian Miller
	Royce Mills
Dalek Operators	John Scott Martin
	Cy Town
	Tony Starr
	Toby Byrne

EPISODES

1) 2-8-84
2) 2-15-84

The Doctor (Peter Davison) and Tegan (Janet Fielding) pose with Daleks on the London docks. © *SUE MOORE*

▶ Story

In the London warehouse district, two fake policemen gun down escapees from a Dalek ship of the future. Two men survive this, Galloway and Stien. They have entered the past down a Dalek time corridor, which is infering with the *Tardis*'s flight. In that future a prison ship is being approached by the Dalek craft, which then attacks. The Daleks and their auxiliary troopers, under the command of Lytton, invade the prison ship. The retreating

THE TELEVISION STORIES

guards attempt to destroy the prisoner that the Daleks are here for—Davros. Lytton's men kill the guards and free Davros from his suspended animation. In the past, Stien finds the Doctor, who is investigating the time corridor. Stien tries to warn him off, but Turlough accidentally triggers the corridor and is catapulted onto the Dalek ship. The Daleks detect the Doctor and send a Dalek into the past to capture him. Army forces commanded by Colonel Archer and helped by Professor Laird come across the Doctor's party just as the Dalek attacks.

On the Doctor's advice, the Colonel shoots out the Dalek's eyepiece. The blind Dalek is then pushed out of a loading door and explodes when it hits the street. Tegan is injured and left to recover. The Dalek from inside the machine attacks one of the troopers before it can be killed. In the future, the Daleks have recovered Davros because they need him. They have lost the war with the Movellans thanks to a Movellan virus that kills Daleks. They need Davros to find a cure—then he can be exterminated. Turlough runs across Mercer and Styles, two survivors of the Dalek raid on the station who aim to prime the self-destruct and destroy it. Meanwhile, Archer is captured by the fake policemen, and when he returns to the injured Tegan

and Laird, he and his troops are acting very oddly, cordoning off the warehouse. The Doctor and Stien have taken the *Tardis* to the Dalek ship, where Stien captures the Doctor.

Stien is a Dalek agent—a Dalek duplicate, to be precise, as Archer and his men are. They are all replacements of originals, but loyal to the Daleks now. The Daleks order Stien to duplicate the Doctor, and he begins the process. Styles has meanwhile managed to arm the prison station's self-destruct, but Lytton's men attack and kill her and her party first. Davros, knowing that the Daleks are only pre-

Tegan (Janet Fielding) and the Doctor (Peter Davison) meet the exhausted Stien (Rodney Bewes). © *SUE MOORE*

tending to obey him, uses a mind-control device to start recruiting troops for his side in the struggle to come. The Doctor learns from Stien—who is becoming more and more human all the time—that the cylinders in the warehouse that attracted Archer and his men in the first place are samples of the Movellan Dalek-killing virus, kept where they cannot harm the Daleks. In the warehouse, Archer casually kills professor Laird when she attempts to escape, then sends Tegan to the Dalek ship for duplication.

When she arrives, however, she is saved by Turlough and Mercer, the only ones who survive there outside of Dalek control. They go to look for the Doctor, who has been freed from the duplication process by Stien. Stien has regained his mind for now, but it may not last. Lytton is losing his patience with the Daleks, and knows that if they deem it expedient they will have him killed. The Daleks have meanwhile realized that Davros is plotting his own takeover, and order his execution. The Doctor beats them there, arriving with Mercer and Stien. He plans to kill Davros but is stopped when Davros offers to redesign the Daleks. While the Doctor hesitates, troopers kill Mercer. Stien, fearing his control is going, heads for the self-destruct chamber to take the Daleks out. Davros arranges to destroy the surviving Daleks, and gives the Doctor the slip.

The final battle begins on several levels. Davros has sent two altered Daleks—redesigned to serve him—into the past to capture the *Tardis*. The other Daleks dispatch Lytton and his men to destroy the renegades, then send Daleks after him to kill him when he has succeeded. On the station, Davros's loyal troops are exterminated, but Davros releases the virus, which begins killing the Daleks. The Doctor again reaches the past, where he, Turlough and Tegan release the virus to finish off the Daleks there. On the prison station, Davros discovers that the virus works on him as well, and he begins to die—then Stien finally triggers the self-destruct and the prison and the Dalek craft are destroyed. In the past, the Doctor and his companions survey the wreckage. Tegan has had enough of all the killing and elects to stay behind. The only other survivor is Lytton, who walks off into London disguised as a policeman, with his two thugs for an escort.

▶ Behind the Scenes

Davros was back now for his third story—and was again played by a different actor! This time, he was looking

THE TELEVISION STORIES

How to destroy a Dalek.
© SUE MOORE

even more the worse for wear. The old Davros mask was slightly redesigned to look even less likely, and the old chair trundled out, with hasty repairs and a fresh coat of paint.

The Daleks—having lost rather badly in the Movellan war—were now using both human troops and duplicates of humans to help them. The human troops had a nice touch, in that their helmets had Dalek eye-sticks, and little sensor-discs on their sides. Their leader, Lytton, would return the following year in "Attack of the Cybermen," where he would be killed off.

The Daleks for this story were all built fresh, for the destruction wrought

on the last of the old ones in "Destiny of the Daleks" left none in usable condition. This time one of the old Dalek shells was used as a mold to create new fiberglass versions. (These included the silly doweling sticks from the old Daleks.) For this story a number of Daleks in various stages of breakdown were constructed. When the Daleks were destroyed at various points during this story, some of their inner workings were exposed along with a nasty mess that was the Dalek creature itself. Oddly, one of the embryonic Daleks seemed to survive quite well outside the casing for a while, even though this had in the past been established as impossible. When the Daleks were destroyed by the virus at the end, they all sprayed out foam and collapsed.

The English version of this story was shown as two fifty-minute episodes, but when marketed in America it was broken down into the more traditional four twenty-five-minute episodes. Curiously, episode two in this format was left without any music or sound effects! It makes for amusing viewing, seeing the Doctor and others rushing about clicking guns and generally acting without the noises that should be there!

Location shooting for this tale took place not far from Tower Bridge—in the same area that parts of ''The Dalek Invasion of Earth'' were filmed.

An interesting scene in this story was the one in which the Dalek mind-scanner was working on the Doctor. The screen in the background showed a regression through all his previous incarnations and companions. These went all the way back to William Hartnell and his original three companions, mostly through the use of stills that were slightly refracted for the view-screen to make them seem like memories floating to the surface of the Doctor's mind.

14. REVELATION OF THE DALEKS

Written by	Eric Saward
Directed by	Graeme Harper
Incidental Music	Roger Limb
Special Sound	Dick Mills
Production Manager	Michael Cameron
Production Associate	Angela Smith
Production Assistant	Elizabeth Sherry
Assistant Floor Manager	Jo O'Leary
Film Cameraman	John Walker
Film Sound	Steve Gatland
Film Editor	Ray Wingrove
Visual Effects Designer	John Bruce
Video Effects	Dave Chapman
Vision Mixer	Dinah Long
Technical Coordinator	Alan Arbuthnott
Camera Supervisor	Alec Wheal
Videotape Editor	Steve Newnham
Lighting Director	John Babbage
Studio Sound	Andy Stacey
Costume Designer	Pat Godfrey
Makeup Supervisor	Dorka Nieradzik
Designer	Alan Spaulding
Script Editor	Eric Saward
Producer	John Nathan-Turner

CAST

The Doctor	Colin Baker
Peri	Nicola Bryant
Kara	Eleanor Bron
Jobel	Clive Swift
D.J.	Alexi Sayle
Davros	Terry Molloy
Tasambeker	Jenny Tomasin
Orcini	William Gaunt
Bostock	John Ogwen
Grigory	Stephen Flynn
Natasha	Bridget Lynch-Blosse
Takis	Trevor Cooper
Lilt	Colin Spaull
Computer Voice	Penelope Lee
Vogel	Hugh Walters
Head of Stengos	Alec Linstead
Mutant	Ken Barker
Dalek Voices	Royce Mills
	Roy Skelton
Dalek Operators	John Scott Martin
	Cy Town
	Tony Starr
	Toby Byrne

EPISODES

1) 3-23-85
2) 3-30-85

▶ Story

The *Tardis* lands on Nekros, where the Doctor wants to investigate the apparent desire of Stenglos, an old friend, to enter suspended animation. The Doctor suspects something is going on. A meeting with a deformed mutant that Peri kills to save the Doctor confirms this suspicion. Stenglos's daughter, Natasha, has the same suspicions and forces Grigory to accompany her to look for her father's body in the vaults. Meanwhile, at the local protein factory, Kara and her secretary, Vogel, are making plans to dispose of the Great Healer. They have employed a Knight of the Grand Order of Oberon, Orcini, and his squire, Bostock. The Great Healer is the one behind all events on Nekros, having taken control of Tranquil Repose, the mortuary. He is none other than Davros.

Davros has lured the Doctor here to begin his revenge. He is using the frozen people as a source of two things: heads and bodies. The bodies are converted to protein for Kara's factories, to feed the starving worlds nearby. The heads are being treated—as Natasha discovers—to become Daleks, loyal only to Davros. Orcini is pleased with the prospect of killing

The Doctor (Colin Baker) with Davros's new Daleks.

the love-infatuated Tasambeker, and Davros assigns her to kill him. She eventually does, before in turn being killed by the Daleks. Takis and Lilt inform the Daleks on Skaro of Davros's whereabouts and they send a ship to capture him.

Orcini's attack on Davros fails, and Bostock is killed. Davros has his Daleks kill Vogel and bring Kara to him. Confronted with the proof of her treachery, Kara has to confess that she planned the death of Davros—and Orcini. Annoyed, Orcini kills her. The Doctor and Peri are captured, but before Davros can wreak his revenge, the real Daleks arrive and take Davros prisoner for trial on Skaro. Orcini still has his bomb, which he triggers, destroying the Dalek incubation chambers. The Doctor and Peri manage to escape along with Takis, Lilt and a few others. The Doctor suggests that Takis use local flowers as an alternative protein supply. Davros has again avoided destruction, but is being taken back to Skaro for trial.

Davros, a being abominated throughout the Galaxy. He is being set up by Kara and suspects this, but he doesn't really care. He is on a mission. Meanwhile, at Tranquil Repose, the people in charge dislike the control Davros is wielding, preferring things the way they were before he arrived. Jobel, the vain supervisor, manages to annoy

▶ Behind the Scenes

The final Dalek story to date takes up shortly after the end of the previous tale, with Davros and the Daleks still

THE TELEVISION STORIES

at odds. Davros is attempting to breed a new race of Daleks from human heads. The Daleks loyal to Davros have a new paint scheme—gold on white—but are otherwise the same as the old ones.

For some odd reason, Davros is seen only as a head for most of this story, but this is apparently just a lure. Orcini destroys it in his attack before the real Davros shows up back in his old chair. No explanation is given as to how the virus that had "killed" him in the previous story did not do so. No explanations are given, either, for Davros using the head decoy. Nor are we told how Davros suddenly acquired the power to shoot electrical bolts from his fingers and from the glass eye in his forehead. For the first time, the same actor, Terry Molloy, returned to play him.

Sound quality in this story is extremely poor. Much of what Davros says is garbled, unintelligible, or hidden by music. The Dalek voices are squeakier than before.

One nice touch is the use of a glass Dalek. One had been planned—as has been noted—for the very first story. Due to expenses it had never been constructed. Here, the heads are grown into Daleks inside a glass shell. Immobile, the structure is apparently only an incubator.

The concept behind Tranquil Repose is one that exists in real life. People are currently being frozen cryogenically to be thawed, theoretically, in the future. It is hoped that at some point a cure for whatever killed the person will be discovered. As this story points out, there is really no incentive for future generations to do this. They will already have enough population of their own and won't need more sick people to heal. Nor will they have any economic incentives to awaken the dead—after all, of what conceivable use would they be to the future? They will be hundreds of years out of date and training. They will be paupers (their money having been spent to keep them frozen, or having been squandered by heirs). What could they do if awakened and cured? All of these are valid points to consider.

CHAPTER
4

THE
DALEK MOVIES

• DOCTOR WHO AND THE DALEKS (1965)

Produced by	Milton Subotsky and Max J. Rosenberg	Editor	Oswald Hafenrichter
		Production Manager	Ted Lloyd
Executive Producer	Joe Vegoda	Assistant Director	Anthony Waye
Written by	Milton Subotsky	Camera Operator	David Harcourt
Based on the BBC TV		Sound Recordist	Buster Ambler
Serial by	Terry Nation	Continuity	Pamela Davies
Directed by	Gordon Flemyng	Wardrobe	Jackie Cummins
Music	Malcolm Lockyer	Makeup	Jill Carpenter
Electronic Music	Barry Gray	Hairdresser	Henry Montsash
Director of		Camera Grip	Ray Jones
Photography	John Wilcox, BSC	Associate Art	
Art Director	Bill Constable	Director	Ken Ryan

Doctor Who (Peter Cushing).

CAST

Doctor Who	Peter Cushing
Ian	Roy Castle
Barbara	Jennie Linden
Susan	Roberta Tovey
Alydon	Barrie Ingham
Ganatus	Michael Coles
Dyoni	Yvonne Antrobus
Temmosus	Geoffrey Toone
Antodus	John Bown
Elyon	Mark Petersen
Other Thals:	Ken Garady
	Michael Lennox
	Virginia Tyler
	Bruce Wells
	Sharon Young
	Nicolas Head
	Jack Waters
	Jane Lumb
	Martin Grace
	Harry Wyler
Dalek Operators	Bruno Castagnoli
	Michael Dillon
	Brian Hands
	Robert Jewell
	Kevin Manser
	Eric McKay
	Len Saunders
	Gerald Taylor

Set Decorator	Scott Senior
Construction Manager	Bill Waldron
Sound Editors	Tom Priestley
	Roy Hyde
Sound Supervisor	John Cox
Special Effects	Ted Samuels
Special Electronic Effects	Ted Hillman

► Story

The stories of both films follow the television scripts on which they were based fairly accurately for the most part. Only where they differ will plot details be noted.

Doctor Who and his two grand-daughters, Barbara (in her early twenties) and Susan (in her early teens) are reading at home. Susan is studying *Physics for the Enquiring Mind*, while Barbara is reading *The Science of Science*. Doctor Who himself is totally engrossed in the adventures of Dan Dare in *The Eagle*. This Doctor is an elderly eccentric Englishman, who is rather absent-minded. Ian, Barbara's latest boyfriend, arrives. Susan thinks he's a fool, and he does give that impression. He manages to sit on the chocolates he brings for Barbara, and almost wrecks a piece of the Doctor's latest invention, the *Tardis*. This prompts the Doctor to show it to Ian, against Susan's advice. "Anyone can understand science if they put their minds to it," the Doctor remarks. Susan is inclined to make an exception in Ian's case. The *Tardis* is rather a mess, with wires and controls strewn about everywhere. The Doctor fits the component that Ian almost sat on, and the ship is ready for its maiden flight. Barbara arrives and enthusiastically greets Ian, who falls on the starting switch—and they are off.

The story progresses. After the trip to the Dalek city, Susan meets the Thals. For the film, they are blue-skinned beings. It is the Doctor, not Ian, who comes up with the idea of taking Dyoni to the Daleks in order to make Alydon fight. When the party led by Ian jumps the chasm in the cave, Antodus doesn't perish this time—he catches hold of another ledge and is hauled back to safety. When the Thals attack the main city, the Daleks surprise them—part of what seemed to be a rock wall opens, and bright lights dazzle the attackers. The Doctor and Susan are captured. The Daleks are preparing to detonate another neutronic bomb to kill the Thals, but then attacking parties arrive. When the Doctor has told Ian of their problem, Ian stops the count-down by yelling for the Daleks. They fire at him and he ducks, causing them to destroy their own control panel. The Daleks are dead, and the count-down stopped. The travelers say their farewells and set off again in the *Tardis*. Instead of reaching home, they find themselves in the path of a marching Roman legion . . .

▶ **Behind the Scenes**

With *Doctor Who* so high in the ratings, and with strains of Dalekmania breaking out all over England, it seemed perfectly reasonable that a film of the show would be made. Despite the American tradition of turning successful films into television shows, in England the reverse tends to be the case. American writer/producer Milton Subotsky accordingly purchased the rights from the BBC and Terry Nation for the use of three Dalek stories. These were "The Daleks," "The Dalek Invasion of Earth" and "The Chase." (The final film was never made, after the second one failed to be a box-office success.)

Naturally, some changes were in order. A show that works on television and lasts for three hours will not work in the same way in a movie half that length. Much of the complexity of the original tale was eliminated in favor of a more direct narration. The clearest changes were in the main characters. The Doctor was gone and in his place was an amiable eccentric, Doctor Who—a thoroughly British chap, if a trifle absent-minded. He was a grandfather still (to both girls this time), but a far cry from Hartnell's cranky old man. Apart from the producer's desire to tone down the Doctor a little and make him more lovable, this was done for contract reasons. Terry had not written the original *Doctor Who* tale about the origin of the Doctor. That had been done by Anthony Coburn. Thus, when it came time to translate the Doctor to the big screen, a fresh beginning had to be written.

Subotsky elected not to use any of the television cast, feeling that they simply didn't have the right box-office draw. For the role of Doctor Who, he chose popular Hammer horror-film star Peter Cushing. Cushing played against type for the part, and did so very well. Ian was played by Roy Castle, a popular light entertainer and singer of the day. This seemed to cover all types of audiences, and the two worked well. It was something of a shock to see Ian so clumsy, considering the fact that he was the hero of the TV series, but that's show biz.

The Doctor (Peter Cushing) and Barbara (Jennie Linden) help Ian hide inside a Dalek casing.

THE DALEK MOVIES

The Daleks were somewhat altered for the film, to make them look a little scarier. Eight were constructed (the film had a considerably higher budget than the BBC), all with larger bodies than their TV counterparts. They had thicker bumpers on their bases, and squared-off light-bulbs on their domes. (One of these would later be used for "Planet of the Daleks.") Instead of the customary sucker sticks, most of the film Daleks were given clawed pincers. This was a good idea and made the Daleks a trifle more versatile than they had been before. A few retained suckers. Another change was in the "extermination" effect. On TV, this was done originally by simply reversing the film—a negative effect—in black and white. When the series was upgraded to color with the Pertwee stories, this was simply extended. The later Dalek stories had traveling color overlays that reversed just a small section of the screen—more sophisticated technology coming through. For the film, the Daleks simply fired smoke. This presumably killed their victims.

The film did extremely well, first in England and then in the U.S. A paperback edition of the first story—written by David Whitaker—was published in the States, as was a comic-book adaptation of the film. Both are now extremely rare. *Famous Monsters of*

Susan (Roberta Tovey), and Barbara (Jennie Linden) and The Doctor (Peter Cushing) move Ian in an escape bid.

Filmland ran an ecstatic (and frequently inaccurate) account of the film, and everything was set for the sequel.

DALEKS—INVASION EARTH 2150 AD

Produced by	Milton Subotsky and Max J. Rosenberg
Executive Producer	Joe Vegoda
Written by	Milton Subotsky
Additional Material	David Whitaker

DOCTOR WHO AND THE DALEKS

Based on the BBC TV
  Serial by   Terry Nation
Directed by   Gordon Flemyng
Music   Bill McGuffie
Electronic Music   Barry Gray
Director of
  Photography   John Wilcox, BSC
Art Director   George Provis
Editor   Ann Chegwidden
Production Manager Ted Wallis
Assistant Director Anthony Wayne
Camera Operator   David Harcourt
Sound Recordist   A. Ambler
Continuity   Pamela Davies
Wardrobe Supervisor Jackie Cummins
Makeup   Bunty Phillips
Hairdresser   Bobbie Smith
Special Effects   Ted Samuels
Unit Manager   Tony Wallis
Construction
  Manager   Bill Walden
Set Decoration   Maurice Pelling
Camera Grip   Ray Jones
Sound Editor   John Poyner
Sound Supervisor   John Cox

An Aaru Production
In association with
British Lion Films

CAST

Doctor Who   Peter Cushing
Tom Campbell   Bernard Cribbins
Susan   Roberta Tovey
Louise   Jill Curzon
David   Ray Brooks
Wyler   Andrew Keir
Wells   Roger Avon

Roboman   Geoffrey Cheshire
Conway   Keith Marsh
Brockley   Philip Madoc
Leader Roboman   Steve Peters
Thompson   Eddie Powell
Dortmun   Godfrey Quigley
Man on Bicycle   Peter Reynolds
Man with Carrier Bag Bernard Spear
Young Woman   Sheila Steafel
Old Woman   Eileen Way
Craddock   Kenneth Watson
Robber   John Wreford
Leader Dalek
  Operator   Robert Jewell

▶ Story

Once again, the story follows the television plot for the most part, though with a number of points of divergence. It opens with policeman Tom Campbell attempting to stop a jewel robbery and then stepping into the *Tardis* thinking it's a real police box. When he steps out again, he, Doctor Who, Susan and niece Louise are in A.D. 2150. The story continues as before, though without Jenny. David Campbell is obviously not a love interest for Susan this time around, since she's only twelve! The Doctor and Tom are captured and both are to be robotized, until the rebel attack saves the day.

Tom and Louise are trapped on the

saucer and get to Bedfordshire that way. Tyler takes Susan with him, until both are betrayed by the women in the wood to the Daleks. The Doctor travels with David to get there. He alone is betrayed to the Daleks by Brockley, the black marketeer. They all discover that the Daleks are going to use Earth as a mobile raiding base to scour the Galaxy. Doctor Who realizes that the Daleks are using humans for the work because they dare not get too close to the magnetic fields down the mine. Taken to the control center, Doctor Who orders the robomen to attack the Daleks.

The Daleks trap the rebels attacking their ship.

The Daleks drop their bomb but Tom has blocked the shaft, and instead of destroying Earth's core, the bomb releases magnetic forces that drag the Daleks down the shaft. The saucer tries to take off but is in turn sucked back and destroyed. The invasion is ended. Doctor Who then takes Tom back to the robbery from the beginning of the story, and lands a few moments early. Ready for what will happen, Tom manages to grab the robbers after they have struck, thus earning himself a well-deserved promotion.

▶ Behind the Scenes

For the second film, there was absolutely no doubt who the stars really were. The TV show might be *Doctor Who*, but for the second film, the Daleks didn't merely get top billing —the Doctor wasn't even mentioned! The poster confirmed this, with Daleks blasting away at the audience and robomen marching in grim order. The largest word on the poster was *Daleks*. Yet, despite all of this, the second film did not do well. In England it managed brisk business, but the main money to be made was always in the American cinema—and it simply fizzled there. Due to this, the projected third film (based on ''The

The Daleks solution to all problems—exterminate!!

Chase'') was never made.

Despite the somewhat disappointing reception, the second film is in many ways vastly superior to the first. The effects work was excellent, especially the Dalek flying saucer. In the TV show, this was simply a static, standard flying saucer. For the film, it was a unique-looking creation, with spinning windows and fine photography. It looked most impressive, and the model was later reused in another British film, *The Body Stealers*.

As there were to be no more Dalek films, four of the Daleks from the second movie were given to Terry, who housed them in his garage. They were later loaned to Selfridges in London, who wanted to use them for a Christmas display to entice children. Though four were loaded on the truck to take them to busy Oxford Street, only three made it onto display. Somehow an audacious thief managed to make off with one of the Daleks in broad daylight, on one of the busiest streets in London! (Daleks seemed to be prime targets for theft; two on loan to Purple Records in 1972 to promote Jon Pertwee's ''Who Is the Doctor'' single were also stolen! They were apparently later recovered.)

The display at Selfridges drew a huge crowd of children, blocking the street and creating a disturbance. Nothing, it seemed, could calm the children down—until one of the Daleks glided out of the store and demanded that they form an orderly line and behave themselves. The children reacted like rockets, and in moments, they were the quietest crowd ever seen!

Terry's Daleks spent many years ''touring''—appearing at fetes, galas and school events. When he and his family moved to the U.S., the remaining Daleks were given to the Sunshine Home.

THE DALEKS ON STAGE

1. THE CURSE OF THE DALEKS

Written by	David Whitaker and Terry Nation	Bob	David Ashford
		Captain Redway	Nicholas Hawtrey
Directed by	Gillian Howell	Rocket	Edward Gardener
Designed by	Hutchinson Scott	Professor Vanderlyn	John Moore
Daleks made by	Shawcraft Models Limited	Marion	Hilary Tindall
		Dexion	Nicholas Bennett
Produced by	John Gale and Ernest Hecht	Ijayna	Suzanne Mockler

CAST

Wyndham's Theatre. Premiered December 21, 1965, and ran into early 1966.

Sline	Colin Miller
Ladiver	John Line

▶ Story

In A.D. 2179, the starship *Starfinder* is heading for Earth. Aboard are two prisoners, Sline and Ladiver, and Professor Vanderlyn and his assistant Marion. Redway is the commander, Bob is the engineer and Rocket is the copilot. The ship is forced to land on Skaro for repairs. Here they meet the Thals, led by Dexion and his sister Ijayna. The Daleks have been inactive in their city for fifty years, but the humans waken them. One of the prisoners thinks that he can use the "robots" to conquer the universe, but the Daleks plan on doing that alone. The Daleks are defeated for the time being.

▶ Behind the Scenes

This story was actually a sort of link between the first two Dalek stories on television. David Whitaker wrote a short background for the play's program book, which first gave rise to the idea of "The Dalek Chronicles," later used in the *TV21* comic strip. In it, he claimed that Terry had found a small glass cube in his garden containing microfilm histories of the Daleks. Terry had translated them, and hence the tales. They are some form of future history, and other cubes have since turned up, with further tales. This fanciful idea was perfect for children watching the play. As with most plays in London for the Christmas season, it was aimed at a family audience and ran only for the Christmas period. It had been originally intended to run at the Strand Theatre, but the venue was switched at the last moment. It was performed at matinees only, and demand was high enough for the performance to run twice on many days.

2. DOCTOR WHO AND THE DALEKS IN SEVEN KEYS TO DOOMSDAY

Written by	Terrance Dicks
Directed by	Mick Hughes
Designed by	John Napier
Sound by	Philip Clifford
Production Supervisor	Trevor Mitchell

THE DALEKS ON STAGE

CAST

The Doctor	Trevor Martin
Jenny	Wendy Padbury
Jimmy	James Matthews
Jedak	Ian Ruskin
Tara	Patsy Dermott
Garm	Anthony Garner
Master of Karn	Simon Jones
The Emperor	Jaquie Dubin
Marco	Robin Browne
Clawrantulars	Peter Jolley
	Mo Kiki
	Peter Whitting

The Adelphi Theatre, Christmas 1974 (four-week run into 1975), then on tour until April 1975.

Trevor Martin was the Doctor for the stage play.

▶ Story

The Doctor has regenerated and is sent by the Time Lords to the planet Karn. He had been there before, had taken a crystal and been shot from ambush. Karn is a ruined planet, once the center of a great empire. The inhabitants had quarreled and the empire had died in flames. The Doctor now shows his crystal to Jenny and Jimmy, his new companions. They accompany him to Karn. There they meet resistance fighters Jedak, Tara and Garm. The ferocious Clawrantulars roam the planet, but the adventurers manage to find two more crystals—Garm has a second, and the Doctor finds a third in the ruins. There are seven in all, and together they make up the Crystal of All Power.

They head for the city but are attacked by the Clawrantulars, who kill Garm. The survivors head into the city. The computer bank there stores the information that they need. Garm gives the Doctor his crystal. On their way in, they are attacked by more Clawrantulars but the Doctor manages to discover another crystal—four so far. The computer discovers them, and is interested in them. When it finds out that they are looking for the crystals, it shows them that it has one, but was programmed by the Masters of Karn to kill any who try to assemble the Crystal of All Power. It also reveals that one of the Grand Masters still lives. The Doctor confuses the computer, allowing them to escape with its crystal.

The Doctor suspects that the Masters of Karn broke up the Great Crystal to prevent its misuse. Whoever the Clawrantulars are working for wants to reassemble it, and the Doctor hopes to convince the last Master that it is better left with the Time Lords for safekeeping. Jedak gives the Doctor his crystal, making a total of six (though the first is safe in the *Tardis*). The Doctor and his companions now discover that their true foes are the Daleks. The Doctor sends Jedak and Tara off in one direction to try to find the Great Hall, while he, Dave and Jenny head off in another. The Doctor confronts the Grand Master and is forced to fight a mental duel with him for the final crystal. The Doctor wins. The Daleks arrive, wanting the crystals; the Doctor scatters six of them and the Daleks are distracted long enough for him and his friends to escape to the *Tardis*.

The Daleks need the final crystal, and know that the Doctor will try to get the others back. Jedak stages a mock attack to occupy the Daleks. The Doctor manages to kill the guard Dalek and Jenny takes its place in the travel machine, getting them into the Dalek base. Here she is captured and taken to the Emperor Dalek. The Doctor discovers that Tara has been telling the Daleks what has been happening. They have captured her brother, Marko, and threatened to kill him unless she helps them. The Doctor and his companions rescue Jenny and Marko, who knows the Dalek plans. The crystals are to be used to power their Ultimate Weapon, which will drain the living energy from everything except the Daleks. The Doctor slips into the room where it is stored, but the Daleks attack his friends. Marko is killed and the rest captured. To save them, the Doctor is forced to turn over the final crystal, but he has used the *Tardis* to change its molecular structure. The Ultimate Weapon blows up, destroying the Daleks. The Doctor and his two friends escape, with Jedak and Tara.

▶ Behind the Scenes

This play was staged during the TV hiatus between John Pertwee and Tom Baker, so there was little problem in using a new actor for the part. The story opened with only the sound of the *Tardis*, then the lights came up to

THE DALEKS ON STAGE

reveal it. Trevor Martin staggered out, dressed like Jon Pertwee, as if he had just regenerated. Jenny and Jimmy were actually in the audience, and rushed onto the stage to help him—at which point the play proper began.

Sadly for the audience, the play opened during the time that the IRA was making regular bomb threats in London and especially in the theater district. As a result, attendances at plays that Christmas were rather poor.

The Clawrantulars were actually named Crocs in Terrance's script, but the theater held a name-the-monster competition, and the winner suggested the eventual name. Terrance eventually reused a number of the concepts from this story (including the barren world of Karn) in his Doctor Who story "The Brain of Morbius." The search for the crystals was reminiscent of the final Jon Pertwee tale, "Planet of the Spiders," though it was suggested by Terry Nation. The Daleks for this story are ruled by the Emperor Dalek, but it is heard and not seen.

THE HISTORY OF THE DALEKS

The home world of the Daleks is the planet Skaro, the twelfth planet of a solar system not too far from our own. This small world has a single continental body, which covers just over a third of its surface. Small islands and chains of islands dot the rest of the planet, allowing some strange forms of life to proliferate in isolation. Its humanoid race evolved on the main continent, and after the normal rise to the rudiments of civilization, the race split into two separate groups.

Across the rough center of the single continent is a large range of mountains, the Drammankin Range—no real barrier to a technologically sophisticated people, but to the Stone Age tribes of Skaro, virtually impassable. For whatever reasons—long lost in those legendary days—the humanoids of Skaro split, and one faction undertook the long and dangerous trek across the mountains to be on their own on the farther end of the continent. The two groups then grew over the next thousand years in isolation, each knowing of the other but having no contact whatsoever.

The tribes to the west became known as the Thals. Those to the east were initially known as the Dals. After the move, they decided to change their tribal name so that it was dissimilar to that of the Thals. They named themselves after the first letter of their joint alphabet: Kaled. Naturally, the Thals resisted calling them this for as long as possible, since they realized that the Dals were trying to less-than-subtly assert their primacy.

Each group moved on through farming and agriculture until they had built their first cities; they then began the rise to advanced technology. Thal histories went back almost half a million years between the prehistory of the race and the war that almost destroyed the planet. Contacts between the two races were not frequent, and the Kaleds disliked even those few occasions. Their legends told that their ancestors had crossed the mountains to escape persecution, and they resented the Thals having done this to them. The Thals' legends, on the other hand, said that the Kaleds had disagreed with the tribal policies and when they were outnumbered and outvoted, had left to form their own community where they could do as they pleased. They were therefore quite ready to accept the Kaleds back to union—though, naturally, only when the Kaleds admitted that the Thals were in the right.

The two sides grew apart emotionally and intellectually even as they grew closer geographically and technologically. Neither side could allow the other to have superiority, afraid that in such a case they would be overrun. As each side developed atomic power, missiles, and poison gas, the other seemed to gain the same knowledge at roughly the same time. Espionage was rife, since it was impossible to tell Thals from Kaleds in any but ideological ways. As the technological advances continued, mutual suspicions grew, and the state of poor political harmony between the two peoples broke down even further, until an all-out war seemed inevitable.

It was at this point that a Kaled scientist came to prominence. His name was Davros, and he was considered perhaps the foremost intellect of the millennium. His grip of cybernetics, microsurgery and genetic engineering seemed unequaled. His work on grafting mechanical and biological units together was certainly the work of genius. His dedication to research was unparalleled, but he was rumored to be rather too intense and obsessed. Nonetheless, the Kaled leadership could not afford to ignore his brilliance, since his new methods promised ways of gaining superiority over the Thals. Accordingly, he had to be kept isolated from spying activities, and allowed to work at his own pace in the company of similar-minded scientists.

THE HISTORY OF THE DALEKS

The Kaled government decided to build a bunker, hidden from their own people—and, hopefully, safe from the Thals. The Kaled capital lay on the plains below the mountain range, in the center of a large forest, but the bunker was built farther north, closer to the sea. Here the mountains were lower, but the bedrock was solid. The government decided that the bunker could double as a point of safety for itself, should the city be the target of a Thal attack. The lower levels, running like warrens through the solid rock, became the province of the scientific corps, while the upper levels were to be the new home of the government.

The bunker was actually a well-kept secret despite the Thal spies who attempted to ferret out what was transpiring there. The Thal government, worried that the Kaleds might be making advances undreamed of, redoubled their efforts to penetrate the bunker. In the meantime, they began construction of a similar one of their own, an equally well-kept secret. They had a rough idea of where the Kaled emplacement was, and their own bunker, rather ironically, was just a few miles away over a small range of mountains.

One Thal operative finally managed to get into the Kaled bunker. Once inside, he realized just how efficiently the Kaled war effort was pro-ceeding, and he saw that the frontiers of science and technology were being pushed back at a terrific rate by Davros. The bitter, obsessed scientist was working hard, pushing hard, and firing up his staff with both resentment of his moods and respect for his incredible intellect. Davros had originated genetic research aimed at taking some of Skaro's seas' plentiful aquatic

Davros (Michael Wisher), creator of the Daleks.

creatures and adapting them to carry explosives to Thal targets. He had augmented their intelligence, given them new senses, and heightened their endurance. They would be formidable weapons should a war occur. Davros had pioneered work in cybernetics, replacing defective or destroyed body parts with mechanical and electronic equivalents—most of which were superior to their natural counterparts. He had even begun work on laser technology, using ruby crystals to generate beams of terrifying potential.

The spy knew that should Davros continue, the Thals would be swiftly outclassed in the impending combat. He therefore sabotaged one of Davros's experiments, which exploded while the scientist was operating on it. The head of Security apprehended the agent, and, using sophisticated mind-ripping techniques, soon obtained a filmed confession of guilt, including the fact that the man was an agent of the Thal government. This was the final spark that flamed the war. The Kaleds were furious over the infiltration and the assassination attempt; the Thals were embarrassed by the discovery and destruction of their agent. They were also desperately afraid because of the spy's final messages, which indicated that the Kaleds were ahead in weaponry and

research. Both sides attacked almost simultaneously using their latest weapons—neutron bombs.

The capital cities were instantly rendered lifeless. The blasts' terrific heat melted buildings in the centers of the cities, yet left the outer suburbs standing. The forest near the Kaled capital perished and petrified. All living creatures were slain for almost a hundred miles. As the clouds cleared, destruction and death were all about both cities. Neither side had won the first engagement, and both had utilized their only neutron bombs in the effort.

The governments had retreated to their respective bunkers, where they could be safe for the time being. Both possessed a small number of atomic weapons, but had also evolved the defense against such weapons—a type of shielding that could be raised above the bunkers. Two domes were formed into which numerous refugees fled. Shanty-town dwellings sprang up and the unwinnable war continued. Eventually even the atomic weapons were used up, and the fighting went on with tanks, machine guns, poison gas and anything else that could be found. Such was the pace of the war that neither side had the time to excavate for fresh materials. As the spare parts or ammunition for a weapon wore out or ran out, it was discarded and fresh,

THE HISTORY OF THE DALEKS

less sophisticated arms were employed. Neither side considered surrender.

The assassination attempt on Davros had not succeeded. He had been left almost dead: one arm, both legs, part of his chest, his eyes, and a part of his skull had been crushed in the explosion. However, his team had instantly placed him on one of his own life-support systems, hooking him directly into the machinery. Davros was alive, and his condition stabilized. To save him the surgeons cut away the lower portion of his body, and the crippled arm. He was grafted onto a mobility unit he had helped to design that could be controlled mentally; this connected to his brain. In the chair portion were placed two separate life-support systems. One was controlled by his own will and the second was a backup system in case he should ever be rendered insensate. The secondary unit could not keep him mobile, but it could maintain the basic bodily functions until Davros could be revived.

To offset the loss of his normal senses, various mechanical devices were fitted into both the chair and Davros himself as implants. A small photo-electric eye was placed in the center of his forehad, replacing his two damaged eyes. Though his vision was not as fine as before, since it was

no longer stereoscopic, it was augmented. Davros could see into infrared and ultraviolet, making his sight more acute in darkness and bright light. His destroyed larynx was replaced with an electronic analogue; though his voice was mechanical he could still speak. His sense of touch could not be directly replaced, but small units in his chair "bumps" served as radar sensors to enable him to avoid objects and move about freely. His own skin had been damaged by the corrosive chemicals and was now mostly discolored and patchy.

Davros was alive, but he was not as he had been. There was some worry that the accident—or even the solution—might have had vast emotional impact on his bitter but brilliant mind. If this was so, Davros made no mention of it. Instead, he reiterated his desire to return to the work of winning the war for the Kaleds, and promised breakthroughs compared to which all previous scientific advances would be nothing. With the war dragging on, the Kaled government agreed, and assigned him a special guard. Over the years a number of such security commanders kept him safe, though none as fanatically as the final one, Nyder.

Davros had changed in ways deeper and worse than anyone could have suspected. As he had hovered between life and death his mind had tumbled from sanity. He was convinced that he had been almost killed because of the Kaled government's failure to adequately protect him; sometimes he even wondered if they were so afraid of him and his brilliance that they had engineered the attempt themselves. At any rate, he felt that he now owed them no allegiance whatsoever. At best they were imcompetent fools; at worst, conniving would-be assassins. Davros had, while injured, seen what he must do: the Kaleds must be reborn. Only he could accomplish this.

In his studies, Davros had noticed that not all forms of life that had been irradiated by the fallout had died. Some had mutated. What he had been attempting in his laboratory in a small way, nature was performing out on the blasted surface of Skaro on a larger scale. Most of the resulting mutations were so hideously deformed that they died out—but some of them not only survived, they thrived. Davros had a number of these transferred to his own study center deep in the warrens of the bunker. He traced the genetic drift and the changes, but what he wanted most of all was to see the effects upon Kaleds and Thals.

Random scanning of the old capital city showed Davros that it was no longer entirely dead. The metal walk-ways and buildings now housed some of the mutant creatures. Some were mutated animals but many were mutated men crawling back to life as best they could in an environment that they remembered from better days. These Kaled mutations were of a variety of forms, and they were exactly what Davros required. The city was no longer any more dangerous than the rest of the surface, and he and Nyder managed to travel there without being observed. Davros found that his old laboratory was still relatively intact and, after he had restored it, he captured some of the mutant Kaleds with Nyder's willing help. These he experimented upon and dissected, leaving them either dead or to fend for themselves however they could.

He soon learned that the forces of mutation working on the Kaleds were not entirely random. Radiation was changing the genetic pattern, and it would tend to produce a stable end result within a couple of centuries at the most. The end form would be small and wizened, totally unlike the Kaled form, and it would have claws instead of hands. But it would be stable, and it might be able to survive in the radiation-scarred world it would inherit. Davros was fascinated, and began to design a mobility unit for one of these mutations. Since they were clearly no longer Kaleds, he termed them

THE HISTORY OF THE DALEKS

Daleks. This was a clear choice for him, since that was the final letter of the alphabet. *Kaled* had been a claim of primacy on the part of the Dal peoples; Dalek was a claim of completion from Davros for his creations. To him they were the ultimate life-form, and the choice of their name seemed obvious.

Using whatever resources he could in the old capital, he built his prototype design. It was based on his own mobility chair, with life-support and stabilization systems built in. It could be controlled by the creature from within the casing, and its senses were, like his own, augmented. The same sensor discs that his chair used served as prototypes for those of the Dalek machines. A specialized iris and lens system provided them with vision. A sucker-stick type of arm would give them the ability to hold and use materials. For armament, they used a variation of his own ruby laser-beam projectors.

The end result of this work pleased Davros immensely. The Daleks he had created resembled—in a twisted way—the children he could never have. They were his creation, the fruits of his genius, and the inheritors of his vision of the future. These primitive casings were simply the beginning, as far as he was concerned. Since the city was almost dead, it had very little power available. Davros

Davros (Michael Wisher) used his own chair as the basis for his "Mark Three" travel machines—the first true Daleks.

had been forced to use simple static electricity to power these casings, with the Daleks moving on a single large roller that acted as pickup for the power with which he electrified the floors. It was primitive but it served for the moment, and that was all that mattered. Once he was back in the bunker, he aimed to refine the design, adding a small internal power pack and external solar-powered cells to make the machines independent.

This had all been conducted in utmost secrecy, because Davros was not insane enough to think that the Kaleds would approve of his experimentation. Now that the preliminary work had been done, he abandoned the city and returned to the dome and bunker to work in earnest on the creation of his Daleks. With the added resources of the bunker, he could make far more sophisticated fighting machines, and also work on creating his Dalek beings from embryos instead of waiting for natural causes, which would take decades. He was able to begin this work, convincing the Kaled rulers that he was breeding them the ultimate fighting machines that would enable them to win the war. In fact, he was working toward his own ends, subtly changing the genetic makeup of the embryos he had fertilized, eliminating what he considered to be weaknesses in the Daleks—emotions such as pity, compassion, love, and mercy. His ultimate race would inherit the universe, and needed to think of no others. He bred into them a fierce loyalty to their own species and taught them contempt of all others—including the Kaled race from which they had sprung.

Davros neither knew nor cared what would happen to those early Daleks he had created and then left in the old capital city. His mind was on other matters, and he simply left the shells and his hasty notes within the depths of his old laboratory, unaware of what the future would hold for them . . .

Once he was back in the bunker, Davros began work on his travel machines. These would be far more sophisticated versions of the Dalek casings he had created in the old city. The new casings (termed the Mark 3— his own being Mark 1, and his initial Dalek designs Mark 2) worked with several different power sources, allowing them greater mobility and not restricting them to the static electrical power their prototypes used. A ring of solar cells was constructed about the midsection of the casing. In cases of need, there would be a battery pack inside the casing. An optional addition—useful for overcast areas—was a small dish that could be attached to the back of the Dalek to collect broadcast power.

Davros used chemical agents to change Kaled embryos into Daleks. Though a number of the scientific elite disagreed with what he as doing, they could not openly attack his policies. Notable among them was one of the chief researchers, Ronson, who believed that Davros was creating

THE HISTORY OF THE DALEKS

monsters utterly devoid of conscience.

But Davros was not alone in his vision. The Time Lords of Gallifrey had also seen the potential within the Daleks. With their own methods of scanning time and space, they saw the danger that the embryonic Daleks could wreak. They felt that this was too great a threat to intelligent life, and elected to use their rather reluctant agent the Doctor to stop the creatures' development. "We foresee a time," their spokesman informed the Doctor, "when [the Daleks] will have destroyed all other life-forms and become the dominant creatures in the universe . . . we'd like you to return to Skaro at a point in time before the

Harry (Ian Marter) and the Doctor (Tom Baker) are captured by the Kaleds.

Daleks evolved . . . [to avert their creation] or affect their genetic development so that they evolve into less-aggressive creatures." This was a challenge that the Doctor could not ignore. Despite the fact that this was a point at which the Daleks were being created, he had met and battled them many times previous to this in his own tortuous existence in the time stream.

This was the critical stage in the Thousand Year War. In fact, the war itself had lasted only a quarter of that length of time, but the politicians liked the ring of *Thousand Years*. It enabled them to glorify their struggle into epic proportions—as if a mere 250 years of warfare had not done enough damage! Both sides were ludicrously short of soldiers and materials by now, fielding armies that consisted of young men, hardly more than boys for the most part. The armies were both very badly underequipped and overworked. The four miles that separated the Kaled and Thal strongholds were wormed through with trenches. Poison gas floated through the polluted air and silences were broken by occasional barrages of shells. If war is hell, then Skaro had become an outlying region of the netherworld.

Despised and slain by both sides were the Mutos. These were creatures once human, now badly mutated by the decades of chemical and radioac-

Davros!

itics and logic are not often too compatible, and no one really worried about the matter. They simply killed the Mutos when they could. The Mutos favored neither side and simply avoided all fighting whenever possible. They spent most of their time scavenging for anything they could to eat or to make their wretched lot slightly more comfortable.

The Kaled government knew that matters were bad, but they were limited in what they could do. The Kaled people would never accept peace before the Thals were destroyed. Mogran, the leader of the government, was forced to support Davros and the scientific elite, believing them to be his people's only chance of winning the war. If matters were a trifle irregular, they could be overlooked. Mogran was fighting a war in which his chief general—Ravon—was in his early twenties . . .

Then Ronson managed to sneak a message from the bunker to Mogran, thanks to the Doctor. It detailed accusations against Davros that claimed that the chief scientific genius on the planet was not actually working to end the war, but to create mutated forms of the Kaled race. Mogran called a meeting of those in the council who were less than worshippers of Davros. Together they agreed to an investigation of what was actually trans-

tive pollution that had impregnated the planet. Some looked almost normal; others were undergoing bizarre and repulsive changes. Nyder stated the official line when he claimed that killing them was right: "We must keep the Kaled race pure." This was, of course, ridiculous, since Nyder was assisting Davros to mutate the Kaled into its final form anyway! Still, pol-

THE HISTORY OF THE DALEKS

piring below their feet, and issued an order to Davros to cease his work until this investigation could clear or condemn him. Davros, though furious inside, kept his temper and agreed to those insufferable terms, in order to buy himself the time that he needed.

His initial trials with the Daleks were perfect. They were totally under his control, and a force of twenty was being produced. To Davros's delight, the Dalek creature had identified the Doctor as an alien, and its response had been the desire to slay the non-Dalek. The Daleks were everything Davros had worked for, and now those fools in his government aimed to stop him and to close down the production of his offspring. Davros had absolutely no intention of cooperating with Mogran and his weak-spined followers. If they were to learn the truth about what he was doing, Davros was certain they would terminate the Dalek project. He knew that even some of his scientific elite—many of whom he had trained and helped—did not approve.

It was time for the drastic steps that he had long anticipated. It was time for the Kaled race to die so that the Daleks might live.

The Kaleds had designed rockets using distronic explosives; Davros had developed a coating for the Kaled dome that would withstand the dis-

tronic attack. The Kaled spies reported that there was a final effort by the Thals to build one last distronic missile to attack the Kaled city. The Kaled government knew that nothing could come of this attack, and was not worried. It did, however, give Davros the leverage that he needed. With the aid of only the obsequious Nyder—the one person Davros trusted—Davros approached the Thals with a staggering offer: a method to nullify the protection of the Kaled dome so that the Thals could destroy Davros's own people. "My only concern is for peace," he lied. "An end to the carnage that has virtually destroyed both of our races." Wanting to believe this, the Thals accepted his offer. "By dawn tomorrow, our world could be at peace." The peace, naturally, would be that of a Thal total victory.

At dawn, the guns of the Thal forces fired the chemical that dissolved the protection of the Kaled dome. Then they launched their rocket. Unhindered, the distronic explosives detonated and wiped out virtually the entire Kaled race in a single blow. All that survived were those in the depths of the bunker—the scientific elite.

To these shocked and shattered men, Davros offered a hope for revenge and a vision for the future: "We will avenge the annihilation of our people with a retaliation so massive, so merciless it will live in history!'' Everyone was affected, and no one seemed to realize that Kaled history was about at an end. While the mood was high, Davros exposed his greatest threat—Ronson—as a spy, and had his Dalek kill the unfortunate man. ''Today the Kaled race is ended,'' Davros cried, ''consumed in the fires of war. But from its ashes will rise a new race—the supreme creature, the ultimate conqueror of the universe— the Dalek!''

Knowing nothing of this, the Thals naively celebrated their supposed victory. They cheered Davros as a hero even as he gave orders for more alterations on the Dalek embryos. Even Gharman, who so far had stood with Davros in everything, was appalled at the changes he demanded. Gharman could not believe Davros's claim that eliminating the conscience and sense of morality in the Daleks was an improvement. Davros now ordered his strike force of the twenty prepared Daleks into the Thal city to wipe out the fools there. Unprepared for further fighting, and never expecting an enemy within their own walls, the Thals fell in thousands to the Dalek onslaught.

Some survived, escaping into the bleak wilderness. One Thal leader, a woman called Bettan, began to round up as many soldiers as she could.

Overcoming her distaste of Mutos, she persuaded them to join in to fight this new menace. The source of the Daleks was clearly the Kaled bunker. Urged on by the Doctor, Bettan planned to seal the Daleks into the bunker, thereby gaining the Thal survivors time—preferably centuries—to regain some level of civilization.

At the bunker, Gharman and other men, such as Kowell, were worried about the instructions Davros was issuing. Gharman realized that the Kaleds were doomed and that the Daleks had inevitably to take their place. He wanted the embryos to have a sense or morality, a sense of pity—to retain what was most valuable in the Kaled race. Unknown to them, Davros was aware of their planning. Rather than spend his time rooting out each and every traitor to his grand design, Davros aimed to let them show themselves, and then eliminate them all at once.

At this point Davros and Nyder managed to capture the Doctor and his young companions. Davros was no fool, and realizing that the Doctor was what he claimed to be—a traveler in time and space—he demanded from him information about the future of his creation. The Doctor reluctantly gave this, and begged Davros to turn the Daleks into a force for peace. Davros had no use for such a silly

THE HISTORY OF THE DALEKS

Davros (Michael Wisher) was willing to destroy his own race in order to ensure the survival of the Daleks.

the charge. "They are conditioned simply to survive," he explained. "They can survive only by becoming the dominant species. When all other life-forms are suppressed, when the Daleks are the supreme life-form in the universe—then . . . we will have peace. They are the power not of evil but of good." Needless to say, this somewhat partisan position was not one that the Doctor could assent to.

Davros's vision of the universe as the home of only one race—the Daleks—was exactly what the Time Lords were afraid of. The thought was abhorrent to the Doctor, who tried without success to force Davros to stop the Dalek production. Davros recalled the twenty units from the Thal city, in order to strengthen his hand in the bunker. Gharman and Kowell had begun their rebellion, determined to force Davros to make the Daleks moral. Davros had no desire to see his valuable men killed in the fighting, so he and Nyder surrendered, asking to be given a chance to convince the elite of his position. Gharman, still foolishly wishing to believe Davros, agreed. Despite all Davros's plotting, Gharman—like the other Kaleds—had been raised to think of Davros as their savior. It was difficult for Gharman to realize that he was a deadly danger.

Gharman's beliefs were pure idiocy to Davros. "They talk of democ-

thought; he believed that his Daleks could only be powerful through strength, and could only be strong through total repression of other life-forms. The Doctor claimed that the Daleks were evil, but Davros—like all truly evil creatures—could not believe racy," he sneered to Nyder. "Freedom! Fairness! These are the creeds of cowards! Achievement comes through absolute power, and power through strength." Meanwhile, the Doctor had been freed, and determined that his mission was almost a total failure. His only remaining option was the destruction of the Dalek embryo room in the hope that this would eliminate the Daleks. Once there, however, he realized that what he was hoping to do was not ethical. "If I kill," he explained to Sarah and Harry, "if I wipe out a whole intelligent life-form, then I become like them. I'll be no better than the Daleks."

In fact, his crisis of conscience was not as important as it seemed. Davros had already established an automated process for the construction of the Dalek travel machine and the production of embryos. The worst that the Doctor could manage was to delay this for a short while. There was now no way to prevent the birth of the Daleks. As it happened, Gharman stopped the Doctor, believing that the rebels had beaten Davros. The Doctor was freed from his decision. Above the ground, the Daleks began to enter the bunker, ready to help Davros. They were followed by Bettan and her troops, who prepared to seal all the surface exists and emtomb the Daleks, hopefully forever.

Davros had called the survivors to a meeting. He presented his case to the assembly, and lost. The majority favored the reprogramming of the embryos to make them capable of full moral choices. Davros forced them all to choose between his position and that of Gharman. Once the two sides were drawn, the waiting Daleks emerged and slew the faction that opposed Davros and his plans.

In the meantime, the Doctor, Sarah and Harry had escaped the carnage. The embryo rooms were destroyed, but not permanently. The trio made its way to the surface just seconds before the Thals, under Bettan, sealed the passageways. On a monitor, they began to watch the final events transpiring below in the bunker.

What Davros had not anticipated was that the Daleks themselves might not approve of what he had planned for them. They had begun their own production lines, before he was ready. When he ordered them to turn it off, they ignored his commands. When Nyder attempted to implement Davros's order, the Daleks turned on him and killed him. Davros's world was crumbling about him, and he hysterically demanded that the Daleks obey him. Their leader refused: "Our programming does not permit us to acknowledge that any creature is su-

THE HISTORY OF THE DALEKS

perior to the Daleks." Davros should have known this, since it was his own instruction; he had simply never imagined that his Daleks would apply it against him and his scientific conspirators.

Now that they were secure, the Daleks did not need the scientists, and slew them, despite Davros's pleas that they could help. "Pity?" the Dalek grated in reply to his creator's imploring. "I have no understanding of the word." Davros had learned too late what the true end result of his own cold, remorseless genius would be. He was the final victim of the Dalek fire, which was meant to kill him. Yet, even as he had underestimated the power of his creations, they in their own turn had underestimated his powers. His primary life support was destroyed but his backup system still worked, maintaining his life and beginning the repairs to his body that might take centuries to finish. The Daleks simply shunted his "corpse" and that of the other Kaleds into a side room and sealed the room—forever, they believed.

Bettan and her Thals had entombed the Daleks, but this was a temporary measure at best. The small party's last sight of the Daleks showed the leader encouraging its fellow Daleks: "We are entombed, but we live on. This is only the beginning. We will prepare. We will grow stronger. When the time is right, we will emerge and take our rightful place as the supreme power of the universe!" With this dreadful promise ringing in their ears, the small group of Thals and Mutos headed into the wilderness to try to start a fresh life for themselves.

For the next few hundred years, life was far from easy. Bettan's small band moved away from the war-ravaged zones only to discover that almost the entire surface of Skaro was polluted. They finally found a tiny strip near the coast where, with much hard work, crops could be raised. Bettan managed to organize her followers into a community where all refugees were accepted, without regard to their background. Life was hard, but the group began to make it.

The mutations that had begun continued, but in a different direction than the Kaled mutations. Instead of remaining decaying caricatures of their former selves or evolving toward the hideous Daleks, the Thals evolved toward physical perfection. Bettan's folk became tall, strong and handsome people, and the Thals were a reborn race. They were, however, pitifully small in numbers, and their fertile land was meager.

Alydon, the Thal (John Lee) meets with Susan (Carole Ann Ford) in the petrified forest.

The band remained very conscious of its history. Bettan had learned from her experiences that warfare was suicide, and had taught that only through nonviolence and peace could the Thals become strong. The children of Bettan's band carried her message down through the centuries, and the Thals became a totally pacifistic society. These gentle people were vegetarians and lived simply, for the planet could support nothing more than the most meager of life-styles. As the years passed, they prospered and grew in number. They kept full records of the history as it was known, but their

knowledge of the Daleks was blurred. The name of the Kaleds was lost because of the horror that the original colonists had felt for the Dalek machines. Over the centuries the Daleks came to be thought of as the enemies the Thals had fought—though none living knew what a Dalek looked like.

The Thals thrived, and this caused the next problem. The land was still badly polluted from warfare. As the population grew, food became harder to find. Finally one leader, Temmosus, realized that the only way for his people to survive was to seek out new lands and new food sources. Temmosus was a direct decendant of Bettan, and he had inherited her courage and vision. Along with a young relative, Alydon, he assembled a small group of pioneers who would venture back into the war zones to attempt to find cultivatable lands and new food sources for the Thals.

Meanwhile, the old Kaled capital had been resettled. As Davros had predicted, the Kaleds caught on the periphery of the original neutron bomb explosion had mutated into the form that he had termed a Dalek. Seeking refuge and help, these pitiful creatures—as they completed the chain of mutation that would leave them dying and crippled—migrated back to the

THE HISTORY OF THE DALEKS

city that their ancestors had fled. Once there, they discovered the remnants of Davros's experiments.

His original travel machines—powered by the city's energy sources—stood empty. The old capital had been drawing its power from the nearby lake, and it still generated the peculiar form of static electricity that Davros had required for those travel machines. When the mutants crawled into them, they were powered up and ready to move. To the mutations, these machines were clearly designed by their ancestors for their own use. They had evolved their own myths about the war, since they had long been out of touch with other intelligent beings. They knew, however, that they had once been something other than the crippled beings they had become.

Some of Davros's notes were intact, and so these creatures discovered that they were Daleks. They learned of the war with the Thals, obviously their hereditary enemies. They explored the city and brought it back to life. The last surviving wild mutations they condemned to the lake behind the city, the Lake of Mutations. The city was theirs again, and it grew as their power grew. It blossomed in the wilderness as further sections were opened and repowered. Still, the city was vast and underfilled. Huge areas remained empty.

The Daleks needed their travel machines to stay alive and to protect themselves from the radiation, they thought. This last they had garnered from Davros's notes, not realizing that they were in fact products of that radiation, and thus immune to its otherwise lethal dosages. They planned some day to free themselves from the machines and reclaim their world. Besides the travel machines, the Daleks needed food, so they experimented with several concepts. Some notes led them to try hydroponic growing, which proved successful. Little nutritious food could grow in the irradiated soil of Skaro. What could grow were lethal monstrosities, such as the Varga plants. These, the Daleks soon discovered, thrived on Skaro's soil—and could move about and infect other creatures, converting them into replicas of the Varga. Naturally, they could not penetrate the Dalek casings.

The Daleks were actually developing into fine scientists over the century or so that it took them to reclaim and remake the city of the Kaleds. Their minds, honed by bitterness and the desire to rebuild, evolved into terrible tools. They could never be certain that any of the Thals had survived the war—but if any had, they would be ready . . .

* * *

The Thals had built their home in an area where there was very little rainfall. This had saved the soil there from the pollution suffered by virtually all the rest of the planet. The problem was that the ground was consequently very dependent on the huge storms that occurred about every four years. The storms were never predictable, and at this point, they failed to materialize at all. The ground became more arid, the crops fewer and fewer.

Opinion was divided on what should be done. Temossus maintained that simply waiting and hoping for rains was foolishly optimistic. Their only chance was to find a better food supply elsewhere. In answer to this, his opponents (in their gentle Thal way) pointed out that he would have trouble finding any food sources that were not polluted or lethal. Temmosus's opinions, however, won the day when starvation became a serious threat. The Thals had developed a drug that could help them survive in the irradiated areas of the planet. It was an extract of one of the radiation-resistant plants. They stocked up enough to last them for several years, trusting that they would find food on the way.

The Thals set out through the wastelands of their once-beautiful world. They carried their historical and scientific records, and what items of the old technology they had salvaged over the years from the dead cities of the past. They were not a large group even now—barely two hundred, all told—but they were strong, they were brave and they were determined. They traveled for almost four years, managing to live scantily off the land as they sought out better food supplies. These were nowhere to be found, nor were there traces of other survivors. Perhaps the Thals had been expecting none, but all the same it was a terrible blow to learn that they shared their world with just the few animals and plants that were about— and countless mutated creatures that none could name.

They worked their way toward the old Dalek capital, and finally the advance guard moved out to scout the area. Alydon, the natural next in line for leadership, took a small party of the younger men into the petrified jungle that lay close to the city. Ganotus—a cheery, reckless type— and his brooding brother, Antodus, took four Thals and headed for what the old maps showed to be the lakes. There they encountered a terrible view of the changes that had overcome their world. The once fresh lake was now rank, and it abounded with mutated creatures that preyed on any living thing. Of the group, only the two brothers escaped alive.

THE HISTORY OF THE DALEKS

Susan (Carole Ann Ford) and the Doctor (Wiliam Hartnell) find themselves captives of the Daleks.

Meanwhile, in the forest, Alydon had made a very strange discovery. There were other beings alive there—four in all—but they did not seem to be Thals, nor did they match his people's legends of the Daleks. Curious, he followed the four and tried to speak with the young girl in the group. She panicked and ran from him. He followed the visitors back to the tall blue box that they were apparently camping in, though it looked very small to contain them. Wanting to make amends, he left a gift to show his good will: a box of the anti-radiation drugs. When the strangers saw them, he conjectured, they would see that the Thals were sophisticated and civilized.

The four travelers were the first Doctor, his granddaughter Susan, and the teachers Ian and Barbara. Not realizing what the box was for, they simply left it inside the *Tardis* and set off to explore the city that lay beyond the forest. Unknown to all of them, the Daleks had been monitoring the activity in the forest, through their rangerscopes and vibration detectors.

When the intruders arrived at the Dalek city, they split up to search. The Dalek council was pleased, for this gave them the opportunity to examine one of the people. Were they Thals? They certainly didn't look like Daleks, so what else could they be? Had the radiation induced this mutation in them? They selected Barbara as their first captive, because she was alone

Prisoners of the Daleks.

and apparently unarmed. By using their monitors and closing off doors behind her, they trapped her in an elevator and brought her below the city to the inhabited levels. There she was captured and briefly examined.

The intruders seemed weak, and the final three were also taken without incident. The intruders seemed sick, and undoubtedly needed their anti-radiation drugs to survive. The council was interested in the drugs because they were well aware of the ties that limited them to the city. They wanted to get out and reclaim their world, but they could not live for more than a few moments outside of their travel machines. If they could get the Thal drug and use it, they could escape their confines. Accordingly they interrogated the oldest of their captives, the evident leader of the group. To him they explained their belief that he was not a Thal:

"Over five hundred years ago, there were two races on this planet: we, the Daleks, and the Thals. After the neutronic war, our Dalek forefathers retired into the city protected by our machines. Most of [the Thals] perished in the war, but we know that there are survivors. They must be disgustingly mutated, but the fact that they have survived tells us that they must have a drug that preserves their life force."

THE HISTORY OF THE DALEKS

The solution was obvious once the Doctor realized that the container outside the *Tardis* was a sample of the drugs: the Daleks insisted that Susan fetch them. She was the only one well enough to travel alone into the forest. The Dalek council, however, had absolutely no intention of letting the prisoners use the drugs—which they wanted for their own experiments. The prisoners would be simply allowed to die once their usefulness had ceased.

In the forest, Susan collected the drugs from the *Tardis* and then met Alydon. Though scared at first she calmed down, and accepted him as a friend. Alydon was surprised to hear that the Daleks were still alive, but it gave him hope: presumably they would have food, perhaps enough to share. He explained to Susan the Thals' need for food, and she promised to try to help. When she admitted that she did not trust the Daleks, he gave her a second set of the anti-radiation drugs in case the Daleks kept the first. He then gave her his cloak for protection. Susan returned to the city and informed the Daleks of what had happened. Since there were two sets of the drugs, the Daleks allowed Susan and her companions to have the duplicate set to cure themselves. Clearly, these prisoners might yet have their use.

The council was elated to realize that the Thals now in the petrified jungle were the last of their race. If they could be wiped out, the Daleks would have their world to themselves. The means was obvious: food. The Thals wanted it, and the human captives wanted to help the Thals. The Daleks could offer food as bait to draw in the Thals, and then exterminate them all. They had been monitoring the captives and announced to them that they would help the Thals, "which is what you want us to do." Susan was easily duped into writing the note for the Thals—then she realized that the Daleks were intending it to be a trap.

In the forest, the next party of Thals caught up with Alydon and Ganatus. Temmosus heard with pleasure the news that the Daleks still lived; he hoped peace could be made between the Thals and their old enemies. Ganatus was less confident. Alydon admitted that he trusted Susan and believed she meant them only good. His opinion of her influenced his opinion of the Daleks' message, and the Thals decided that they would accept the invitation from their old foes to share their food surplus.

In the city, the four prisoners managed to break the cell monitor so that they could talk without being overheard. The Daleks were not too worried about this, believing their captives to be helpless. This foolish confidence in their own superiority would cost the Daleks dearly. The guard assigned to feed the prisoners was overcome and killed when the Doctor realized that the Daleks depended on their strange form of static electricity to survive. Disguised as the Dalek, Ian managed to get the four safely into an elevator. The Daleks soon detected the escape, however. To stop Ian, the council had simply to magnetize the floor, rooting his Dalek to its spot. Other Daleks then burned down the door to the elevator shaft, but not before the prisoners had made good their escape.

Other matters now pressed on the council, for the Thals were approaching the city, walking into their trap. Temmosus insisted on being the first to enter, and made an impassioned plea for peace and cooperation to rebuild their dead world. Ian had doubled back and saw that the Daleks were paying no attention to the speech. He cried out a warning and the Thals retreated. Several of them were left behind when the Daleks opened fire. Temmosus was the first to die. The rest of the Thals retreated to safety in the forest, gathered about the incongruous shape of the *Tardis*. Alydon was promptly declared the new leader, and all of them wondered why the

Daleks had tried to kill them.

Ian had the answer: "A dislike for the unlike." The Daleks were totally xenophobic, and would not rest until all other races were subjugated or dead. The Thals simply could not grasp such monstrous horror, and resigned themselves to simply giving up and moving on. Ian tried to make them understand that sooner or later the Daleks would find a way to leave the city and come after them. As long as the Thals lived, the Daleks would never rest. He believed that they simply had to fight, moral scruples or not. Alydon was not so sure. "Look at our planet," he explained. "This was once a great world, full of ideas and art and invention. In one day it was destroyed. And you will never find one good reason why we should begin destroying everything again."

In fact, Alydon was wrong on two counts. The destruction of their world was the work of more than a single day; the destruction of the city and the forest was perhaps what he meant, since they had been the first casualties of the war. Also, Ian had found a very good reason for the Thals to fight—survival. By threatening to take Alydon's bride to be, Dyoni, to the Daleks as a sacrifice, he provoked Alydon to punch him. Alydon *knew* that Ian was doing this, yet he was filled with fury when his Dyoni was

THE HISTORY OF THE DALEKS

threatened. All night long he considered the problem of whether or not they would fight to help Ian and the others and to save their own people. Finally, with the dawn, he decided: the Daleks left them no option but to do battle.

They had no way of knowing it, but the fight had become critical. The Daleks had tested the Thal anti-radiation drugs and discovered that they were lethal to the Daleks. The Daleks were not only used to radiation; they now needed it to survive. The exterior radiation counts were dropping, a condition that would mean the end of the Daleks. The council decided on the obvious: "We do not have to adapt to the environment; we will change the environment to suit us." Since it would take too long to build and detonate a second neutron bomb, the Daleks decided instead to vent the waste from their nuclear-power generators into the atmosphere. This would raise the radiation level to a point at which even the drugs could not help the Thals to survive.

Ganatus was quite ready for Alydon's decision to fight. Showing keen tactical sense, he proposed an expedition try to approach the city from the rear, by way of the Lake of Mutations. This horror-filled swamp had cost the lives of several of his friends and had terrified his brother, Antodus. How-

ever, the Daleks were using this as a barrier to guard the rear of the city, and would never expect an attack from that side. A small party might be able to make it through the mountains and gain entry covertly. Alydon agreed to this, giving them three days to make the journey. Along with the two brothers, Ian, Barbara, Elydon and Kristas would make this dangerous journey.

The swamp was a nightmare, and Elydon was dragged under and devoured by some half-seen creature. The rest of the party made it through to the mountains, where they saw the pipes for the Dalek city vanishing into the mountains. The Daleks clearly had a way through the range—perhaps a tunnel. The searchers finally found a way through, though Antodus was still terrified. Their way was eventually blocked by a chasm, which had to be jumped. Ian acted as an anchorman for the others. Antodus was the last to jump, and panicked, falling into the chasm. His weight dragged Ian down, despite all that Ganatus could do. Seeing this, Antodus bravely severed the rope tethering him to Ian. Ian was saved but Antodus plunged into the chasm to his death.

In the meantime, the Doctor and Alydon had not been idle. Using mirrors they had managed to confuse the Dalek monitoring devices—and believed that they could safely approach the city to sabotage the entire system. The Daleks, however, had vibration detectors planted under the streets and could track the Doctor, Susan and Alydon when they entered. Alydon returned to the forest to alert his people to the attack, and the Doctor began his sabotage. Unfortunately he enjoyed his moment of triumph too long, allowing the Daleks to capture him and Susan. Here the Daleks explained that they were ready to deflect the radiation from the reactors to kill the Thals: "Tomorrow we will be the masters of the planet Skaro."

In the cavern, the small party despaired—until they found the entrance to the city. Now they could begin their work to help the attack. In the forest, Alydon roused his people for the assault on the city, little knowing just how critical matters were. The Daleks were almost ready to begin the venting process when the twin Thal assaults struck. The Doctor had been attempting to bargain with the Daleks, offering them the secrets of his time and space machine if they would spare the Thals. The Daleks refused to bargain, aiming to take the machine and use it anyway once the Thals were dead. The movement of the Thals was detected, and the Daleks began sealing off the city corridors.

A small party of Thals managed to get through to the central control com-

The end of the Daleks?

plex. Here a brief but vicious fight began, and ended only when the Thals destroyed the power controls. All electrical power in the city died, sealing the doom of the Daleks. "Stop our power from wasting," the council leader begged the Doctor. "Or it will be . . . end of Daleks." The Doctor had no idea how to restore the power, and the Daleks all died. Alydon grimly

THE HISTORY OF THE DALEKS

surveyed the scene. "The final war," he muttered. "If only there had been some other way."

In fact, he was being overly optimistic. This was far from the final war; the Dalek menace had hardly even begun to stir.

With the city now in Thal hands, Alydon discovered that they could use a great deal of the Dalek technology for their own purposes. Especially useful were the hydroponic gardens, enabling his people to feed themselves. The Doctor and his friends continued their strange journeys, leaving the Thals to peacefully take over the Dalek city and adapt its technology to their own uses. The Thals prospered. Alydon married Dyoni. The race began to grow again. For five hundred years, there was peace on Skaro. The surface radiation died down in almost all areas, and it began to be possible to consider replanting the surface. It looked as though the Thals had finally regained a fine world.

In the city they made great strides, studying the technology of the Daleks. They built and flew their first spacecraft, and were actively looking into the possibility of inhabiting other worlds. Their histories told them of the Doctor and his friends, so they knew there was life elsewhere, waiting to be found. Unfortunately, there was also other life on Skaro, and it did not intend to wait any longer. Five hundred years of peace were over.

The Thals had begun to plant in the soil of Skaro. Various exploratory parties had mapped out the planet but all had avoided the two old bunkers from the Thousand Year War. No one had wished to approach them too closely, once they had been identified as the reminders of that long-finished madness.

Under the Kaled rubble, however, the Daleks were ready.

They had been planning their return. They had perfected underground mining systems, which automatically delved for the metals that their automated production lines needed. Left alone with the vast embryo banks, the Daleks had built up their numbers. They had honed their warfare techniques, studying the computer records that had been entombed with them. They were now prepared to take on whatever might remain on the surface of their world.

The original leader of these Daleks had set up a chain of command. He was the Dalek Prime, his casing painted in gold to distinguish him. Under him came the Dalek Supreme, also known as the Black Dalek from the paint on his casing. The Black

Dalek was the warlord of the race; and below him were dozens of minor ranks. Red Daleks were section leaders. Red-and-gray Daleks were transportation, and the rank and file were simple gray and blue. The life supports built into the Dalek casings meant that no Dalek would be forced to die a natural death for several thousand years. The later Dalek embryos, however, had been implanted with obedience to the original Daleks, and would gladly die to further the Daleks' purposes. Die they would over the centuries, but they would kill even as they died. All were still fired with that implacable hatred for all other forms of life—especially any humanoid lifeforms that reminded them of what they themselves had once been.

Into the peaceful Thal world, the Dalek invasion force erupted. A huge swath of death was sliced again across the face of Skaro, much of it before the bewildered Thals even knew that they were under attack. The Black Dalek led his forces into action, annihilating all who opposed them—and any who simply tried to escape. In a matter of hours, most of Skaro was a burning cinder.

Once again, however, the Thals survived. With the initial attack, the Thal starships still close to the world returned. They collected what survivors they could find, and whatever

could be salvaged before the Daleks destroyed their society. They then fled, leaving the Daleks as the masters of Skaro. The world was uninhabitable again, after all the Thals' efforts. The overcrowded evacuation fleet staggered across space to one of the colony worlds that the Thals had been experimenting with. Now they had no option but to trust to this planet for their survival as a race. With the arrival of the ragged fleet, the Thals vowed that never again would the Daleks take them by surprise. Pacifism was no longer foremost in the Thal mind; instead, they determined that they would somehow, someday, utterly destroy the Daleks.

The Daleks themselves knew nothing of this, nor would they have cared. They had cleansed their world of the Thals, believing that it was forever and that the small remnant that had escaped would soon die out. Should the Thals survive, they would be found and destroyed. Skaro finally belonged to the Daleks alone; now it was time for the rest of the universe to follow.

For a hundred years or more, the Daleks prospered. They rebuilt their capital, eliminating from it all evidence of the Thals. The city grew as they raided the old bunker for equipment, computer systems, and metals. Finally the remnants were buried, as the Daleks sought to conveniently for-

THE HISTORY OF THE DALEKS

get the fact that they had been forced to spend five hundred years lurking below ground while their enemies had prospered. Their capital expanded and they had access to the accumulated knowledge of the Thals in the computers they discovered.

The Dalek Prime thus found out about starflight. Since the Thals had had no warning of the attack, all of their plans and propulsion methods were laid out in detail in their records. The Daleks had been experimenting with antigravity, building discs that could contain a single Dalek and support it in the air, controlled mentally by the creature within the casing. Utilizing these principles and the Thal knowledge, the Daleks pieced together a hybrid starship. This was tested, proven successful, and then used as the basis for a fleet.

Despite the fact that Dalek embryos were produced through cloning, the Dalek numbers still remained fairly small. Skaro was almost exhausted, worn out from the wars, and it contained too little metal for the Daleks' purposes. What they needed was another world that they could mine. It had to have plenty of metallic ores, and preferably abundant radioactive elements that could be taken fairly simply. It had to be a world in which they could move about. If it had a native species, so much the bet-

ter—they could be used and then destroyed.

The Thal deep-space telescopes were still in orbit above the planet. The Daleks used them and finally discovered exactly the place they were looking for: Earth.

It was A.D. 2164 on Earth. Finally, Earth was more or less united under a central government. The exploration of the solar system was well under way. Lunar bases dotted the crater surface of the Moon, and a Transmat system linked the world and its natural satellite. This was in itself not such a good thing, for the use of conventional rockets and spacecrafts was dying out. Why spend days in a tin can when you could walk through a booth and appear on one of the lunar bases?

Earth was experiencing a time of prosperity. Many cities had installed moving pavements, curtailing private transportation and freeing towns from congestion. Cheap fusion power provided convenient energy augmented by huge orbital satellites that gathered the energy of sunlight and broadcast it to a waiting Earth. Weather control was beginning, and it looked like a new age of peace and expansion was under way.

Then came the meteorite bombardments. Scientists theorized that Earth was passing through cometary debris—though it was puzzling that it hadn't been detected before this. The falling showers caused minor damage, but on the whole it was more spectacular than dangerous—until the plagues began. For millennia, superstitious souls had believed that portents in the sky had marked the onset of plagues. Mankind had grown beyond such foolishness—except in this case, that was exactly what had happened. The meteorites had been seeded with a virulent plague developed by Dalek research. The Daleks did not have the numbers to attack and defeat the combined military might of Earth, so they had approached the problem obliquely.

Over those terrible months there were billions of deaths. Scientists and doctors worked on the killer plague and finally managed to effect a cure—but it was far, far too late. The world had split assunder again, into small communities. Plague victims had been cremated whenever possible, or simply dumped into the nearest river (which was forbidden, but done anyway). Normal services had ground to a halt, economies collapsed, and the whole structure of human society died. Those poor souls isolated on lunar stations starved slowly; the Transmat terminals on Earth were in-

"We are the masters of Earth!" The Daleks with the Houses of Parliament.

operable, and the lunar operatives could not return home.

Animals were not affected by the plague. In the initial months of the infestations, a great number of animals escaped from zoos or were released by sympathetic humans. Many thrived in their new situation. Alligators lived in the old sewers. Lions prowled New York streets. Packs of once-pet dogs combined to hunt outside the cities. Humans had to struggle against nature to survive. Cities began to decay mere weeks after the plagues began.

Then the Daleks came. They sim-

THE HISTORY OF THE DALEKS

ply razed some cities, which they never could have held, and occupied those that could prove useful. The human communities were too small to fight back individually, and too far apart to band together and counterattack. Resistance groups sprang up, but with very little success. The Dalek casings were impervious to normal fire power, but the Dalek guns were extremely effective against humans. There seemed little the humans could do other than evade Dalek patrols and try to stay alive. That wasn't easy to do.

The Dalek forces were spread very thin. There had only been a dozen of their saucers in the first place, and the total invasion force numbered no more than five hundred. They were commanded by the brilliant Black Dalek, whose grasp of strategy made even the strongest human counterattacks quite futile. Captured humans were experimented upon and the Daleks began to augment their forces with humans. The Daleks knew about the electromagnetic fields around each living brain, and had discovered a method of manipulating these temporarily, creating a condition of utter obedience in the victim. They could then be completely dominated by electronic pulses channeled through a radio receiver in a headset. The Daleks called these human automatons robomen—half robot, half men. The only drawback was that the continual interference with the natural brain functions invariably led to mental breakdown, madness and death. This was an inconvenience, since they then had to be replaced.

These robomen aided the Daleks in controlling strategic areas of the world. The Daleks had no real interest in the human race beyond a malicious glee in humiliating them. The humans reminded the Daleks of their own lost heritage, and the invaders enjoyed working their captives to death in menial, foolish chores, or converting them to robomen. Robo patrols kept the resistance fighters out of the way for the most part, and they also rounded up fresh workers. The plan was for the invasion force to turn Earth into a gigantic starship and pilot it back to their own solar system, where it could be exploited for the much-needed metals and radioactive elements.

Accordingly, the Daleks probed the surface of the planet. They discovered that a huge fault lay just a few miles below the Bedfordshire countryside in England. It could be reached by a mine shaft and then split apart by a small nuclear charge. This would enable the combined Dalek saucers to extract Earth's precious molten core. In its place they could install huge

The Daleks were everywhere on the conquered Earth—even in the Thames!

generators to pilot the planet. The core could be cooled and exploited, since it was almost pure iron and radioactive elements. The only problem in this was that the molten core also produced large magnetic effects, which the Daleks could not get too close to without damage to their internal computers and other life-support systems. The bulk of the work would have to be accomplished using robomen and slaves.

Since this was taking place in the English countryside, the Daleks concentrated many of their forces there. London, the obvious place to occupy, became their central receiving station. The old Chelsea Heliport was made into a saucer landing site. The fleet of ships was used to transfer prisoners from all over the world here for robotization or transport to the mines in Bedfordshire. The small English resistance groups knew all of this, but could do little. The robomen patrols and the Dalek forces hunted them down, attempting to annihilate them.

Not all humans resisted the Daleks, of course. Some actively collaborated with them, trading information and other humans for food. Others, convinced that the Daleks would be defeated eventually, looted cities or they traded food for valuables from the prisoners in the camps. As in all such situations, some of the most

THE HISTORY OF THE DALEKS

undesirable people managed to flourish for a while.

Into this situation the *Tardis* arrived, bearing the first Doctor, his granddaughter Susan and the teachers Ian and Barbara. Unaware of what they were getting into, the four were soon plunged into the thick of the war. Susan and Barbara were found first, by the resistance, and taken to their cramped headquarters below the Elephant and Castle subway station. The resistance fighters were led by the crippled genius, Dortmun. He dreamed of fighting back and had spent years perfecting a bomb that he believed would penetrate the Dalek casings. The action leader was a tough, cold man named Carl Tyler. A younger man, David Campbell, still retained much of his humor and enthusiasm, but it was leaching out fast. Jenny, the only female of authority, was a total cynic. With them were about twenty fighting men—not much with which to take on a Dalek invasion force.

The Daleks viewed the resistance groups as more of a nuisance than a danger, but even minor irritations had to be dealt with. The Black Dalek made regular broadcasts offering amnesty and work to any rebels who surrendered. "Resistance is useless," he explained. "We are the masters of Earth." To encourage defection to

their side, the Daleks warned that otherwise "you will all die: the males, the females, the descendants." Daleks, naturally, could view children as nothing else, since they had nothing themselves in the way of family life. The broadcasts had no effect on the resistance members other than to annoy them. "Obey motorized dustbins?" Dortmun sneered, voicing their common opinion. They would never have accepted the Daleks as their masters. Dortmun knew that what the fighters needed was a victory that the Daleks could not ignore, and he spoke out in favor of an attack on the London saucer, using the new bombs. Tyler was more cautious but was stung into action by Dortmun's snide comment: "You've been down here so long you're beginning to *think* like worms."

The Doctor and Ian were not so fortunate. They were both captured by roboman patrols and taken to the Dalek saucer. Both were amazed to see the Daleks again, and the Doctor attempted to rationalize their reappearance after their apparent destruction. "What happened on Skaro was a million years ahead of us in the future," he guessed. "What we're seeing now is about the middle history of the Daleks." The Doctor was simply guessing, and he was guessing incorrectly. Even Ian could see that these

Daleks were far more sophisticated than the ones they had previously faced. On the other hand, Ian had by now learned not to contradict the Doctor!

The Daleks needed a continual supply of robomen, so they tested each batch of prisoners, selecting those of higher IQ for robotization. The process sapped the minds of the victims, so the higher the starting intellect, the better the resulting robo-man. The Doctor managed to find a way out of the cell, ending up back in Dalek hands and slated for robotizing. Before this could be completed, the rebels launched an attack on the saucer with Dortmun's bombs.

The bombs failed to work properly, but they did create a certain amount of confusion for a while. Some of the rebels managed to get into the saucer and free the slaves. Then the Daleks counterattacked, driving the resistance fighters out and annihilating them. The raid was a costly failure, leaving the resistance broken and many of its members dead. The Daleks were furious, for even this failed attack was the worst setback they had received. All of their captives had been freed, even if many were killed attempting to escape. It set a bad precedent, and the obvious answer was to ensure that nothing like it ever happened again.

The Dalek Supreme decided that the best thing to do was to destroy London. A large number of fire bombs was placed about the city, and the Daleks pulled back their patrols and all robomen. There was a final skirmish with the resistance members as these humans tried to leave the city. Some made it, but others—including their leader, Dortmun—were slain. Once the Dalek patrols were aboard the saucer the ship took off and the fire bombs were triggered. Some failed to detonate, but large areas of the city were enveloped swiftly in the conflagration. The saucer moved to the Bedfordshire mining area, where its mission was coming to a close.

Shortly after the saucer landed, the Black Dalek took control of the operations. The saucer moved out to destroy a truck that the rebels were using to escape from the burning city, then it began to gather in all of the patrols from the country. The Dalek shaft had now reached the level of the natural fault in the planet, and the penetration explosive was prepared. The Dalek Supreme contacted all of the other saucers scattered across Earth. They were to move to the mine area and prepare for the delicate task of freeing Earth's molten core. The explosion would be timed to go off shortly after they were all in place.

Across the globe, the Daleks be-

THE HISTORY OF THE DALEKS

gan pulling out. Freedom fighters in the other countries were puzzled by this move, little realizing that the final act in the Dalek plan was being played out deep in the English countryside. The Daleks had no interest in conquering the humans, and even less in enslaving them. They were simply an inconvenience that had to be controlled while the real work was being done.

What the Daleks did not know was that once again the Doctor and his friends were preparing to deal a fatal blow to their plans. Ian had managed to reach the mine. The Black Dalek

Jenny (Ann Davies) and Barbara (Jacqueline Hill) are captives of the Daleks in their control area.

had released a Slyther to patrol the grounds at night. This horrible creature, one of the mutations from Skaro, had two complete digestive systems and two voice boxes. It was huge, shapeless and virtually indestructible—and ate anything it could. No prisoners dared to try escaping at night, because the Slyther hunted by scent and never gave up on a meal. Ian almost became a victim but was saved by leaping into a large crane bucket. The Slyther tried to follow, but fell to its death down the shaft.

The Daleks had by now readied the penetration device. Ian had accidentally chosen the bomb as a place to hide, and he delayed matters for a while by sabotaging it. This was no more than a minor setback that was soon repaired. Ian realized the Daleks were about to drop the bomb down the shaft they had cut, so he blocked the tunnel. When the bomb was released, instead of falling to Earth's core it was trapped a bare five hundred feet below the surface. Unaware of this, the Daleks prepared to abandon the mine, leaving behind all of the robomen and the human prisoners. Barbara and Jenny had attempted to penetrate the control room and turn the robomen against the Daleks, but they had failed. They were imprisoned there, and left to die with the rest of the humans.

The Doctor, Susan, Tyler and David arrived at this crucial point. Some Daleks still remained at the mines to prevent last-minute attacks, so the Doctor had Susan and David destroy the ground power bases that fed these Daleks, killing them. He then freed Barbara and Jenny, and together they turned the robomen against the remaining Dalek forces. Ian joined them, and they all abandoned the area before the final explosion.

The Black Dalek did not really care. Once the core was freed there would be nowhere for the fugitives to escape to—most of England would be destroyed in the catalysm. His ship was recording the images from the control room below, including those of the Doctor and his companions. The other saucers were closer to the site, ready to magnetically grapple the core when it was released.

Then the penetration device exploded. Instead of venting its force against Earth's core as planned, the main shock wave rose upward, shattering the Dalek mine complex and annihilating the hovering saucer fleet. The only survivor—badly crippled—was the Black Dalek's ship. Impotently, the Dalek Supreme watched the molten end of his invasion as full volcanic fury was unleashed below him. There was nothing that he could do but order the return to Skaro—slowly—and report failure to the Dalek Prime. With him, though, he took the footage of the Doctor and his companions.

Earth was left in the hands of the humans again, but their war with the Daleks was not yet over. The last survivors began to repair their broken world and to regain their technology. Forced to improvise, they managed to rebuild their cities. Within fifty years they were strong again.

On Skaro, the Dalek Prime was furious but recognized that there was little that could immediately be done. It was time to take a different and less costly approach to gaining the materials needed. Accordingly, the Daleks began a massive attack on their own solar system. Piece by piece, they started slicing into the nearby moons and planets. They drained them of materials, destroying them as worlds, and used these materials to begin the construction of the greatest army the Galaxy had ever seen.

The Dalek Wars were about to begin.

It took the Daleks several hundred years to build up their army of assault. They had spread to neighboring solar systems, mining the planets for materials. In so doing, they committed a

THE HISTORY OF THE DALEKS

grave tactical error, underestimating the Thal resolve: they neglected the defenses of Skaro. Since their world was worn down they had no particular attachment to the place, and assumed that this would be true of others. The Thals, however, were grimly determined to regain their home world, and they managed to launch an assault from their colony planets back at Skaro.

Because of the Dalek laxity, the Thals managed to seize their planet back again, destroying for the moment all Daleks based there. This effort severely crippled the Thal war efforts, for they were still basically a peaceful people. They knew, though, that they would never know peace until the Daleks were destroyed. They felt a deep guilt that part of the blame for the creation of the Daleks rested upon them, and they vowed to sweep the Galaxy free of their enemies. Accordingly, they began to develop deep-spaceships of their own, ready to strike and cripple the Dalek forces whenever they could. In the captured computer files, they discovered details of the Dalek communications system, which they modified so they could monitor their foes. They then discovered that the Daleks were maintaining a secret base on the planet Spiridon.

The Thals had no deep-spaceships that had been tested, so a volunteer

The Daleks on Spiridon.

crew for a suicide mission was selected to fly to Spiridon, uncover the Dalek plans, and stop them. This expedition would consist of seven, commanded by Mira. Second in command was Taron, the ship's doctor. The ship made the flight but crashed on reaching Spiridon. Mira and three others were killed. Taron, Vaber and Codal, the expedition's science officer, all survived, only to find themselves on a nightmare world.

Spiridon's vegetation was terrifically aggressive, often virulently poisonous. It had forced the intelligent race of the planet to evolve its own defense—invisibility. It was this secret that the Daleks were seeking. They had bombarded the planet with bacterial agents (as they had in their invasion of Earth), killing most of the population. Few survived, and most of those were used for experimentation by the Daleks, or as slave labor. Some of the natives, including one called Wester, tried to fight back, rather ineffectually. The Thals were forced to skulk around, trying to work out the best way to use their few remaining explosives to halt the Dalek plans. Vaber hated this approach, preferring to attack frontally—a suicidal concept to Taron's way of thinking.

What the group did not know was that the situation was even worse than it looked. The invisibility approach was one thing, but ten thousand Daleks were ready to be mounted as an army from this planet. Spiridon had a curious nature as a planet. Ice existed in a bizarre allotrope here—a sort of slushy liquid that was intensely cold. The planet produced this somehow in a natural way—probably due to some enzymic reaction with the plant life millennia ago. Vast rivers of this ice water flowed below the surface, giving the planet a chill surface except in direct sunlight. The Spiri-

dons had tapped into these vents to cool their cities. The Daleks used the vents to power huge refrigeration chambers into which the ten thousand Daleks were placed. They were thus kept cryogenically alive, waiting to strike unsuspected at the heart of the Galaxy.

The Thals on Skaro managed to intercept a call from the Dalek Supreme Council—the advisers to the Dalek Prime—mentioning their army. Worriedly, they dispatched a second ship to Spiridon to warn the first expedition. This ship also crashed, due to the pilots' inexperienced handling of the controls. Rebec (Taron's girlfriend), Marat and Latep were the only survivors, linking with the earlier expedition. At about this time, the third Doctor and his companion Jo Grant arrived.

The Daleks had been planning their strategy for the deployment of the army. The humans on Earth had risen to a position of some power since the defeated Dalek invasion. They had managed in the five centuries since then to build up a small but powerful empire. Close to them stretched another empire, that of the Draconians. Allied, they could weaken or perhaps even defeat the Dalek forces. Accordingly, it was important for the Daleks that the two empires fight. At this opportune moment, the Master had vol-

THE HISTORY OF THE DALEKS

unteered his services. Like the Doctor, the Master had fled Gallifrey, home world of the Time Lords. Unlike the Doctor, he served his own aims, which generally involved gaining personal power. He had seen a perfect chance in helping the Daleks.

With the aid of the Ogrons and a hallucinogenic device, the Master had struck at human and Draconian ships. He had convinced each crew that the other race was attacking, and matters had escalated to the satisfying point of war. This was when the Doctor and Jo had arrived and managed to get the two sides to see the truth. The threat of war between Earth and Draconia was prevented, but the Doctor still wished to deal with the Dalek army. He followed the Daleks to Spiridon, and then teamed up with the Thals there. Together they planned to stop the Dalek experimentations.

Unknown to them, the Daleks had another project under way—the creation of a virus that would kill all forms of life. The Dalek section leader in charge of the project and his chief scientist manufactured the virus and an antiviral agent. They were both immunized, but before they could immunize the rest of their forces and the Spiridon slaves, Wester managed to break the vial in the secure room. He perished instantly, but his sacrifice was not in vain. The two Daleks were

safe from the virus, but if they attempted to leave the room, it would kill every other Dalek on the planet, including their army. They were forced to remain where they were, forever.

Meanwhile, the Doctor and Codal had been captured by patrols and taken to the city for interrogation. They managed to escape and were joined by several of the Thals who were trying to break them out. Marat was slain in the attempt and the others were trapped in the refrigeration unit. They all escaped up the waste heat ducts to the surface. Having discovered from this expedition the layout and plans of the Daleks, the Doctor and the Thals planned an attack. The Doctor believed that breaching the walls of the refrigeration unit would cause the ice to flood in, forever sealing in the Dalek army.

The Dalek Supreme then arrived to take command of the operation, since the Supreme Council was worried about the delays. The invisibility experiments were completed and the Daleks had now gained a method to become invisible for short periods of time. The Dalek Supreme ordered the awakening of the army, preparatory to invading the Galaxy. The Doctor managed to plant a bomb, and flooded the army chambers with the ice. This rose swiftly, spreading throughout the city. Only the Dalek Supreme and two others escaped the rising frozen tide. They then discovered that the Thals had stolen their ship, stranding them on the planet for the time being. "We have been delayed—not defeated," the Dalek Supreme observed. He ordered a relief ship and planned on freeing the trapped army below him as soon as possible.

* * *

The footage of the Doctor and his companions taken on Earth proved to be very curious. The person referred to as the Doctor was clearly the same person whose arrival had been filmed in the old Kaled capital five hundred years earlier. The Dalek Prime replayed the section of the records where the old humanoid claimed to

THE HISTORY OF THE DALEKS

be able to travel through time and space in a device he had used to arrive on Skaro. It was unthinkable that any one person could live five hundred years, and get from Skaro to Earth without the Daleks knowing of it; the only possible answer seemed to be that the Doctor was telling the truth.

If time travel was possible, then the Dalek Prime wanted to use it. He ordered research into the subject to begin at once. This Doctor was clearly a problem for the Daleks, and it would be more than expedient to dispose of him and his companions. The only possible way to do this was, obviously, to build a time machine and track him down. In the meantime, there was much to do.

The first matter for the Daleks was the removal of the Thals from Skaro. Although they had no sentimental attachment to their home world, they could not afford to have the Thals established there, forming a second front to attack them. To the Dalek Prime, the simplest solution seemed to be the mass bombing of the world, rendering it lethal.

As before, the Thals learned of this plan by monitoring Dalek communications. They knew they had no chance at all of stopping the Dalek attack, so they resolved to abandon Skaro again. To prevent the Daleks from realizing that their foes had fled, a small number of Thal troops remained behind to stage a fairly convincing defense of Skaro. It was quite literally a suicide mission, buying time for the Thal race to retreat and consolidate, to fight another day. The small band of volunteers fought long and hard, but the massed Dalek firepower won through. The Daleks dropped several neutron bombs on the Thal settlements, not realizing that the settlements were already abandoned. All that mattered to them was that Skaro was once again free of Thals.

The time-travel program instigated by the Dalek Prime finally achieved results. At tremendous effort and cost, the Dalek scientists built a single working machine. They found that when the laws that controlled operations in time and space were applied, they created stressed space within the device. The interior of the ship was in a different dimension than the exterior, allowing it to be larger than it appeared. The time machine was equipped to track disturbances in the space-time continuum, then to lock in and follow the trace.

The Black Dalek immediately ordered an assassination group to be prepared. The *Tardis* was detected leaving the planet Xeros, and its path locked into their own detectors. It was heading for the planet Aridius, and the Dalek squad was dispatched to intercept the Doctor and his companions and kill them.

Aridius was an old world in a very troubled state. Originally the natives had been amphibians, for the world had once been covered by a large, deep ocean. They had built cities in the sea beds, and developed an advanced culture. Then something had interfered with their planet's orbit, sending it fractionally closer to its twin suns. The overall planetary temperature rose slightly, and the oceans began to evaporate. Over hundreds of years, the oceans literally evaporated into space. Slowly the native lifeforms perished, until only two species remained. The world turned to sand and dust under the relentless glare of those terrible suns. The Aridians survived by staying within their cities, conserving and recycling all of their water. The air locks that had originally been constructed to keep the waters out of the city now served to keep the precious liquids within.

The other survivors were the mire beasts. These creatures were large, carnivorous octopods, with sufficient intelligence to track down their sole remaining prey—the Aridians. The mire beasts were tough and almost indestructible. Nothing that the Aridians could do seemed to affect the beasts,

The Daleks track down the Tardis, prepared to exterminate the Doctor.

so they were forced to simply seal off any sections of the city into which the mire beasts penetrated. It was a losing battle, and the Aridians were slowly dying out.

Unaware of this, the first Doctor arrived in the *Tardis,* along with Ian, Barbara and Vicki. Ian and Vicki stumbled into the city, and the Doctor and Barbara discovered the existence of the Dalek hunters. The Dalek time machine arrived on the world, and the executioners began their search for the *Tardis.* The search was interrupted by a terrible sandstorm that covered the entire desert in howling winds and changed the face of everything. The Daleks were not badly affected, since

THE HISTORY OF THE DALEKS

they could simply wait out the storm, then burrow out of the sand using their antigravity discs. They then located the *Tardis*.

It had been buried in the storm. Contemptuous of the native race, the Daleks insisted on their help to dig out the *Tardis*. Once this had been done, the helpers were exterminated. Clearly, if the Doctor and his companions lived, they were being sheltered by the Aridians. The Daleks therefore demanded that the time travelers be handed over to them, else the Daleks would destroy the Aridian city. As this would doom the race, the Aridians had little option but to accede to the demand. Before they could, however, the mire beasts invaded their city, and in the confusion the time travelers escaped. One Dalek had been guarding the *Tardis*, but he was lured away by Ian and the Doctor. The travelers then made good their escape.

The squad leader recalled the rest of the Daleks, and they set off in pursuit of the Doctor, tracking the *Tardis* and staying on its path. Their time machine was a trifle more efficient than the battered *Tardis*, and they were bound to catch up with it eventually. The next landing was on Earth in the 1960s. By the time the Daleks arrived, the *Tardis* had left and the only being about was an American tourist named Morton Dill. The Daleks had landed atop the Empire State Building in New York City. Dill found the Daleks highly amusing and hardly realized how lucky he was not to be killed out of hand. Unwilling to spend the time to kill such a fool, the Daleks continued after the enemy time machine, gaining slightly.

The next landing was only a period of time away, still on Earth. The Daleks emerged onto a wooden, sea-going vessel. The humans aboard it were clearly too stupid to know what was happening, and jumped into the sea to escape from the Daleks. The Doctor and his friends had already left, so the Daleks followed—leaving the *Mary Celeste* to its lonely journey into history. The next landing was again only a matter of time away— 1996, in Ghana. Here the execution squad discovered that they were up against foes that were unkillable. They were unfamiliar with human literature, so could not recognize Frankenstein's monster or Count Dracula for what they were. Mistaking them for humans, the Daleks attempted to execute them. The effort failed, for both were actually robotic creations who responded by attacking the Daleks.

The Doctor, Ian and Barbara seized the chance to regain the safety of the *Tardis*, but the Daleks prevented Vicki from following. When the monsters attacked the Daleks, though, Vicki managed to slip into the Dalek time machine undetected. The Daleks were unable to kill foes that had never truly lived and were forced to retreat—their quarry had already escaped anyway.

They were still very close on the Doctor's trail and the flight of the *Tardis* indicated that their next landing would be on the planet Mechanus. The Doctor had proven to be more capable than the Daleks expected, so they determined to utilize subterfuge. They had managed to scan the Doctor many times over the years, and they now applied this information to a fabrication machine. This then produced an exact robotic copy of the Doctor—but one that would obey the Daleks' orders implicitly. Once the two time ships arrived on Mechanus, the Daleks released this deadly android to kill the party from within. Unknown to them, however, Vicki had witnessed its creation, and she warned her companions. When the robot appeared, the real Doctor was able to combat and defeat it.

The planet Mechanus was one of a number of worlds that had been intended in this period for colonization by Earth. It was only marginally habitable, so Earth had employed its then-current tactics of sending in a shipload of Mechonoids to prepare the world

for the colonists. The Mechons (as they were also known) were large, rounded robots that could virtually think for themselves, possessing self-awareness to a remarkable degree. Their rounded bodies could extrude tools required for many tasks, and their computer brains could analyze situations and take appropriate action. Earth had sent out a large number of Mechon ships to various marginal planets to prepare them for colonization.

The colonists, however, never did arrive. It was at this point that Earth entered into one of its periodic clashes with other races, and a war in space ensued. When it was over, many billions were dead, and the pressing need for expansion was felt no more. The Mechonoid worlds were abandoned, though the Mechons knew nothing of this and continued to await the arrival of their masters.

On Mechanus itself, vast jungles covered the surface of the planet. A mobile form of plant, the Fungoids, attacked any kind of animal life, enveloping and eating it. Knowing this would create a problem for colonists, the Mechonoids created a great city on legs that rose over a thousand feet above the jungle. Here, humans could dwell in perfect safety. The city was constructed and prepared, and the Mechons settled back to maintain the

THE HISTORY OF THE DALEKS

place and to wait for the human masters they were certain would one day arrive.

After fifty years, one did—an astronaut whose ship crashed there. Steven Taylor knew nothing of the Mechonoids, and had no idea of what their control codings were. Accordingly, he was kept imprisoned by them, fed and allowed exercise. They would watch him from time to time, but he was not allowed free. They served him even as they kept him prisoner. Then after another few years, the Doctor and his party arrived, pursued by the Daleks. The Mechonoids observed this, at first without interest. Then they realized that the party the Daleks were chasing was composed of humans. Accordingly, they helped the Doctor's group escape—and then imprisoned them with Steven. The Mechons were programmed to protect humans, and they could not allow the Daleks to harm them.

The Daleks were annoyed at this interference. It was clear that the only way they could destroy the Doctor and his friends was by first annihilating the Mechonoids. The rest of the assassination squad was called in, and the defenses of the city broached. The attacking Daleks demanded the release of their prey, and the Mechons responded with violence. In a short while, the two groups were fighting

One of the Daleks' most aggressive foes—the Mechonoid.

bitterly. The Doctor seized his chance to flee the city, and the Dalek and Mechonoid clash eventually destroyed the main supports. In a tremendous crash, the city collapsed to the jungle floor a thousand feet below, destroying Daleks and Mechonoids alike.

Ian and Barbara took the Dalek machine to return to their own time, where they then destroyed the time machine. On Skaro, the destruction of the machine was noted. Little could be done for the moment, for the materials used to construct it were very rare, and it would be decades before a second device could be created—providing something more interesting could not be created in the meantime. The time-travel project was open to alternatives.

This clash with the Mechonoids proved to be merely the first skirmish. There were a number of other worlds where the Mechons waited for humans. The Daleks knew that there would be serious problems should the Mechonoids be allowed to grow in strength. Accordingly, they began to systematically search out and destroy all of the Mechon worlds. The resulting wars were long and bitter, but eventually the Daleks prevailed.

One casualty of the Mechonoid attacks was a small party of Daleks in an experimental capsule that had been testing time warping on their foes. The Mechons had destroyed the ship—or so they had thought. In fact, the forces at play on it had sent the capsule hurtling through time and space. Badly damaged, the capsule crashed on the world of Vulcan, completely drained of power. There it sat for decades, the Daleks inside, not dead but deactivated and surviving on small amounts of power in their life-support systems.

Eventually the world was settled by natives of Earth. A sleeper starship had set there in the opening years of the twenty-first century, and had ar-

rived on Vulcan. The crew opted to begin their dating system from the time they had entered into deep sleep; thus for them this was still A.D. 2010, even though several centuries had passed, and Earth now had more sophisticated and faster ships at its disposal. Unfortunately there were members of the colony who had their own ideas of how things should be

Polly (Anneke Wills) and Ben (Michael Craze) meet the Daleks.

THE HISTORY OF THE DALEKS

run, and they desired nothing more than the overthrow of their Earth-appointed leader, the ineffectual Hensell. The chief plotter was Bragen, the colony's head of security. Quinn, the deputy leader, suspected Bragen's ambitions and requested an examiner from Earth.

At this point the colony's chief scientist, Lesterson, discovered the Dalek capsule in the planet's mercury swamps. He had it taken to his laboratory and proceeded to open it. Since the colonists had been in flight during the Dalek invasion of Earth, Lesterson had never heard of the Daleks, and was not disturbed by the three robotic-looking machines he found in there. Testing them, he discovered that they were drained of power. Aided by Janley and Resno, he began to power up the machine, to see if he could get it working again.

Once again, fate brought the Doctor into play. The *Tardis* had just helped him to regenerate into his second self, and had slipped across the space and time boundaries during this operation. The ship had landed on Vulcan, where the Doctor and his companions, Ben and Polly, were taken for the examiner and his party. The Doctor played along, stalling for time, and was appalled to discover his oldest foes on the planet. Despite his fervent pleas, no one would listen to

him and have the Daleks dismantled. On the contrary, Lesterson insisted on powering one of them up. On awaking, it recognized the first thing it saw as a human, and naturally exterminated him. Resno was thus the first Dalek victim on Vulcan. Lesterson cut the power and the Dalek fell back to immobility.

Lesterson, desperately wanting to be proven right about the Daleks' being useful, took away its gun, convinced that the killing of Resno was an accident. Janley was affected also, but in a very different way. She was one of the rebels and saw the killing machine

Ben (Michael Craze), Polly (Anneke Wills), and the Doctor (Patrick Troughton) discover the secret of the Dalek capsule.

plans to help the humans, and set about diverting power from the colony to the capsule.

Secretly, the Dalek worked and repowered its two companions. Together they used the materials the humans were so naively supplying them with to build a small construction line of Daleks. Stored specimens of embryos were unfrozen and set to growing. Janley, knowing nothing of this, approached the Dalek with an offer of help: the rebels would supply further materials if the Daleks would back their seizure of power. Naturally the Daleks agreed—with no intentions of keeping the agreement once they were strong enough. Everything was working fine, as the Daleks had anticipated.

Lesterson, however, had grown worried, and soon discovered that the Daleks were breeding in the capsule—and that they were armed. Before he could do anything, the Daleks were ready for action. Bragen made his bid for power, having Hensell killed. Before he could take command, though, the Daleks poured out of their capsule, aiming to kill the humans and take over the colony. As the Daleks began their process of murder, the Doctor and Lesterson slipped back to the capsule. The Daleks were still working on power drained from the colony and transmitted through the

as a chance to gain power rapidly. The Doctor tried to have the Daleks destroyed, but his warnings were undercut by the Dalek: "I am your servant," it rasped. Preferring to believe their dreams, the colonists kept the Dalek powered up, and it offered to help the colony by establishing an anti-meteorite shield about the place. Foolishly Lesterson believed it, and gave the Dalek all the materials it requested. The Dalek naturally had no

THE HISTORY OF THE DALEKS

capsule. The Doctor and Lesterson set about reversing the energy flow. The Daleks discovered this and attempted to stop them. Lesterson was killed, but the Daleks were too late. The power drain began, and soon rendered them all lifeless. With the Daleks out of the way, Bragen tried to regain control but was killed by one of his own men, disillusioned with the power bid. Quinn took over the colony leadership, while the Doctor and his companions slipped away.

By the conclusion of the Mechon Wars, the Daleks had developed the Time Vortex Magnetron. This device tapped into the time-space vortex that underlay the observable universe, and allowed the passage of objects using a small hand unit rather than the bulkier time machines. The inherent power of the Magnetron gave rise to several interesting possibilities, one of which the Dalek Prime immediately sanctioned: the reinvasion of Earth through time.

When the Daleks studied the history of Earth, they discovered a curious paradox: the historical flow that had led to their first invasion attempt had somehow shifted. Earth in the twenty-second century—a hundred years after the first invasion attempt—was somehow a postnuclear wasteland. The survivors of the human population were living in small groups, trying to survive. It was a situation that the Dalek Prime found perfect for exploitation, and he ordered an immediate invasion of the planet. The reason this had occured was not important—only the fact that it had, and that it presented the Daleks with a perfect second chance.

This time, though, there would be no attempts to move Earth. With the remnants of the human race to tap for slave labor, they could simply process the minerals needed for Skaro to continue its expansion. To keep the human slave forces in line, the Daleks would raise some of them as overseers, called Controllers. As a police force the Daleks knew that humans would be untrustworthy. There were few enough Daleks to control the planet, so the Daleks imported the Ogrons as helpers.

The Ogrons were natives of a distant world, and were only a step up from brute savages—they could communicate. They had absolutely no initiative of their own, obeying any orders given them implicitly and to the death. This made them perfect for situations where Daleks could not be spared to do the job. There was simply no chance for a human to subvert an Ogron or to appeal for mercy, since Ogrons had no desires, and no emotions that they were not commanded to have.

The reinvasion of the Earth was a simple matter, and the Daleks established factories and mines for the needed materials. They also set up plants to make food pills for the natives, though higher-up humans were allowed more natural foods as an incentive to obey the Daleks. No humans were ever allowed to have too much power, however. Some humans—as humans always did—rebelled against the Daleks. Guerrilla resistance movements tried to fight back, hoping against the obvious facts to reclaim their world. The Daleks knew that this was impossible, but they still worked at eradicating the resistance.

Very soon the resistance workers also came to realize that the Daleks were bound to win. Instead of giving up, as the Daleks had expected, the guerrillas simply changed their plans. Since the Daleks had time machines, the guerrillas' secret members in Dalek factories stole the plans and parts to construct their own machine. The guerrillas intended to strike back through time to the point at which the Dalek invasion had become possible.

This alternate future became possible because of a single incident. By the late twentieth century, the international situation had become extremely tense. Nations prepared to mobilize for war, and sporadic fighting broke

The Ogrons were the servants of the Daleks—at least, as long as they could be useful.

out in Africa and South America. Russian forces poised on the Chinese border, and it looked as though World War III was inevitable. At this juncture an English diplomat named Sir Reginald Styles intervened. His long years of service had gained him sympathetic hearing from many nations, and he convened a peace conference at his home, Auderly House. Delegates from all of the potentially warring nations attended, hoping to end the tension. Instead a huge explosion rocked the house, killing all present.

THE HISTORY OF THE DALEKS

It was believed that Styles was some form of fanatic and had intended to provoke the very war he claimed to be combatting. With the house destroyed, war was inevitable. The world simply tore itself apart. There was continual warfare for a hundred years; almost 85 percent of the world's population perished. The few survivors were at the mercy of the Daleks when they invaded.

Having this foreknowledge, the guerrillas aimed to strike before the event—and kill Styles before he could detonate his bomb. Project Intercept was established, headed by Anat, a strong-minded woman. Under her were Shura, Boaz and a third member.

This last member tried first, but failed to reach his target due to the erratic nature of the rebel time devices. A Controller fixed his location and sent Ogron troopers after him. The guerrilla was wounded, but escaped. In the twentieth century, UNIT troops had been called in to help Sir Reginald Styles. They were aided by the third Doctor, who was then working as UNIT's unpaid scientific adviser, and his companion, Jo Grant. He deduced that the would-be killer was from the future, and managed to contact Anat's party when she came into the past to kill Styles. When the guerrillas were traced, they were forced to return to their own time; the Doctor went with them, hoping to find Jo, who had been transported by accident into the future.

The Daleks were amazed to discover that their greatest foe had somehow managed to turn up again, and they insisted on his capture, interrogation and death. The capture was simple, since he tried to break into one of their factory complexes. The interrogation was more difficult, despite the mind-analysis machine. The Doctor's resistance to the mind-ripping techniques was formidable, and it was all that the machine could do to

The Doctor (Jon Pertwee) and Jo Grant (Katy Manning) try talking sense to a Dalek.

extract the information that he was indeed the same person who had already met and frequently defeated the Daleks. His death was not achieved. The Controller wished to use the Doctor to dispose of the human guerrilla groups, and the Gold Dalek in charge of the invasion attempt foolishly agreed to this. (The Dalek Prime had given orders that if the Doctor were ever encountered, he was to be immediately interrogated and then exterminated.)

Before the Daleks could use the Doctor, the humans invaded the control complex and rescued him. When Ogron patrols were assigned to capture the group, the Controller himself helped the Doctor to escape back to his own time. Furious, the Gold Dalek executed the rebellious human and then personally led a raid back to the twentieth century. The Doctor had realized that the explosion at Styles's house had not been set by him but by the freedom fighters. Their own attempt to inferfere with history had caused this. Paradoxically, they had made the Dalek invasion possible: Shura was still in Styles's house, with a bomb. The Doctor determined to prevent the explosion; the Daleks could not allow this, as it would ruin their own invasion.

The Daleks and the Ogron patrol encountered resistance from UNIT troops, who abruptly evacuated the area. The Daleks forced their way into the house, only to discover that the peace conference had been moved. Shura had been alerted by the Doctor, and once the Daleks were all in the house, Shura detonated his bomb, destroying them. The future returned to the pattern it had originally held. Styles's talks were a success, and the international situation calmed down once again. The Dalek invasion attempt never took place. On Skaro, the Dalek Prime noted the shift in the pattern of the past. There had to be another way to foil the human expansion into the Galaxy.

Before the Daleks could begin considering this, they suddenly found themselves in a terrible position. They had been concentrating all of their forces and energies toward the growing power of Earth and its allied worlds, and now they suddenly discovered that there was a foe from a fresh front. From deeper toward the galactic center came the Movellans— tall, beautiful and humanoid in appearance. They were in fact a robotic race, ruled by calm, strict logic. Millennia before, they had been created by some long-extinct race to serve them. The Movellans had soon discovered their perfection; they were more logical and much better suited to rule. They had overthrown their old

THE HISTORY OF THE DALEKS

The Daleks attempted to find their creator on Skaro.

masters, then established control of all near space.

Movellan power spread, reaching out into freshly explored territory. They inevitably took all non-mechanical races as subject populations, and used them to construct further robotic creations. It was inevitable that in their expansion they should finally encounter the Daleks. The Movellans initially saw the Daleks as merely a cyborg race to be swiftly subdued. They did not realize that they had evolved far beyond being simply organic life-forms within travel machines.

Over the centuries, the Daleks had installed ever more sophisticated computers to be used as adjuncts to their own memories and reasoning. This interfacing between creature and machine had given the Daleks insights and abilities they had never known in the past—but it had also given them a serious flaw. They had become the slaves of their inbuilt computers, unable to operate in any fashion their computer logics did not sanction. While far from robotic, they had become enmeshed in the rigorous network of logic.

The Movellans, being pure machine intelligences, were equally the slaves of logic. The two armies faced off and began analyzing the weaknesses of the other. Both armies, governed by their implacable war computers, vied for the superior position. When one moved, the other countered, and the situation, constantly changing, never altered in essence: the two armies stalemated one another.

The Dalek Prime realized that a situation like this called for more than mere logic. For decades, the two armies effectively neutralized one another, and neither could expand. Both knew that this uneasy peace was giving their enemies time to prepare, but neither dared do anything to disrupt the impasse without a certainty of victory. The Dalek Prime began scanning all of the possibilities recorded within Dalek history, going as far back as his records stretched—even to those initial days of the creation of the Daleks by Davros.

It was then that he discovered that certain records about Davros were classified. Working carefully, he broke through the programming and learned that Davros was not—as had long been accepted—dead. There was the secondary life-support system that could keep his body in stasis virtually eternally. All it would take to revive Davros was a large influx of energy. The Dalek Prime was about to discard this as useless when he realized that this might be the lever needed to upset the balance of power. Davros had had the insight to create the Daleks—the supreme force in the universe. Might he not know the way to defeat the Movellans?

It was worth risking, providing certain safeguards were taken. The Dalek Prime knew that Davros considered himself superior to the Daleks and would inevitably try to gain control of them again. He must seem to have that opportunity. The Dalek Prime ordered the special construction of a small group of Daleks that would take orders from Davros but be fitted with explosive devices that the Dalek Prime could detonate in case of need. Davros would be given an extremely small army to order about, but the Dalek Prime would retain ultimate control.

The computer records on Skaro were incomplete, but this did not matter. The location of Davros was known, and there were sufficient humanoid captives in that area of space to help the Dalek task force dig him out. The ship containing these Daleks and a small number of captives was dispatched for Skaro. Their task was to find and restore Davros, and to convince him that he had full control of the Daleks. Unfortunately, the

THE HISTORY OF THE DALEKS

Movellans had broken the Dalek transmission codes and learned of the mission to Skaro—though not of its purpose. Movellan Central sent a ship after the Dalek task force, commanded by Sharrel. He was ordered to prevent the Daleks achieving their objective by any means possible. If it could be managed, he was also to secure their prize, and use it to tip the balance of power in the Movellan favor.

The Dalek force arrived on Skaro and began operations. Some radiation remained from the final war with the Thals, but little enough that the captives could endure it. They began the clearing of the old Kaled city ruins above the bunker where they knew Davros rested. As soon as they could, they repowered the city. According to the computer records, Davros's primary life-support systems needed actinic light from the general illumination to repower. By the time the Daleks reached the level at which Davros had been abandoned, they hoped he would be waiting for them.

Unfortunately, at this juncture the *Tardis*'s erratic wanderings brought the fourth Doctor to Skaro, with his fellow Time Lord, Romanadrevatrelundar (Romana for short). The Doctor and Romana became separated during the blasting the Daleks were conducting to free the way down to the old levels. At this moment, the Movellan search craft arrived. Sharrel and his assistants Agella and Lan managed to discover the Doctor, and began picking his brains about what the Daleks were up to. They soon discovered that the Doctor had been an opponent of the Daleks for a considerable time, and cleverly followed his lead. Romana had fallen captive of the Daleks, and had been put to work on their digging parties. The Doctor and the Movellans were joined by an escaped worker, Tyssan, and they ventured into the Dalek control in the old bunker to work out their objective.

The Doctor realized that the Dalek maps of the levels were incomplete. From his point of view, the thousands of years that had passed between the destruction of the Kaled city and the present represented but a short period of time. He could remember the path that he and Harry had taken without problems, and knew that there was a faster way down to the level the Daleks were interested in. Accordingly, he and his Movellan allies of the moment reached Davros first.

By this time Davros had awakened from his sleep of millennia. His tissues had regenerated and he was expecting to lead his Daleks to universal conquest. As the Doctor observed, the millennia had not improved his megalomania. The Daleks broke through also, and began their search for their creator. Buying time, the Doctor threatened to kill Davros, and his companions escaped. The Daleks responded by killing several of their captives—none of whom was now needed since the digging was completed. The Doctor, instead of surrendering, countered by threatening to kill Davros unless the Daleks freed the prisoners. Davros forced them to agree, knowing that the Doctor would do it. The Doctor then made his escape.

The Movellans had learned from Romana that the Doctor was an expert in cybernetics. They knew that he might give them the edge they needed to win the war, provided that the Daleks did not escape with Davros. Accordingly, they readied a nova bomb. This would ignite the atmosphere of Skaro and destroy the planet —along with the Daleks, Davros and any others who were left behind. Sacrifices were necessary, and Lan agreed to remain to trigger the device. However, Tyssan organized the freed prisoners, and while the Movellans attempted to get the Doctor to help them, Tyssan's force struck. They were able to remove the power packs of the Movellans and to reprogram them to obey Tyssan's orders. Striking at the Movellan ship, they managed to cap-

Agella (Suzanne Danielle), one of the Movellans.

ture it. They now had a transport off Skaro.

Davros had not been idle. He realized that the Movellans might escape with the Doctor, who could bring them victory in the impending showdown. The Time Lord was certain to realize that the way to win the stalemate was to make some illogical

THE HISTORY OF THE DALEKS

move and strike while the enemy tactical computers were attempting to analyze it. Accordingly, Davros equipped most of the surviving Daleks with bombs he could detonate, and then sent them off to destroy the Movellan craft. Once again he had underestimated the Doctor, who used this opportunity to slip in and confront Davros. One remaining Dalek had been left to guard Davros until a deep-space cruiser could arrive; this Dalek was no match for the Doctor, who blinded and then destroyed it. Davros fought against the Doctor but the Daleks exploded early, leaving the Movellan ship unharmed.

Romana had prevented Sharrel from detonating the nova device, and defused it. The freed prisoners could now return to Earth space. The Doctor helped them to rig up a cryogenic unit to take Davros with them in suspended animation. That way he could neither signal for help nor try any tricks. Once on Earth, he could be tried for crimes against all sentient species.

The trial was something of a formality and Davros was condemned to suspension—to be frozen forever in a block of ice on a prison ship in space. He would be alive and aware, yet unable to move or act. Ostensibly a mercy, it was in fact a living hell. His term of sentence, however, lasted only ninety years, not for eternity.

The Daleks finally lost their war with the Movellans when the robotic race played on the fact that their opponents were still organic beings. Experimenting on captured Daleks, they developed a virus that would kill specifically Daleks (they intended to subjugate the humanoid races for their own use, naturally, and had no intentions of harming them). The virus spread fast, utterly decimating the Dalek population. The last few survivors crawled back to whatever retreats they could and reformulated their plans. The Dalek Prime and his Supreme Council retreated to Skaro once again, to their oldest city. Many things remained to be done, and this latest setback had to be rectified.

The Dalek Prime authorized a number of possible avenues to regain their status. The number of time-travel experiments were increased and would soon provide them with heady fruit. The Dalek Prime himself began genetic experimentation to further develop the Dalek form—perhaps to some undreamed-of goal. Daring trust this advancement to no other Dalek, he was forced to use himself as an experiment. The Dalek Supreme was left to pursue a means of combating the virus. His suggestion was the recovery of Davros, using humanoid assistance. A group of troopers under the command of a mercenary named Lytton offered to accomplish this, and it was agreed. With Davros, perhaps there was hope. Lytton knew his location, and an armed ship was sent to intercept and invade the station.

The attack was a success, since the station had been allowed to degenerate somewhat. Earth and its allies were embroiled in a bitter war with the Movellans. With the Daleks out of their path, the Movellans had moved into the humanoid sectors of space. This was not as simple a matter as they had hoped, and the fight turned

___

Tegan (Janet Fielding) and the Doctor (Peter Davison) attempt to help the hapless Stien (Rodney Bewes). © *SUE MOORE*

against them. Slowly the allied forces of Earth and Draconia pushed back the Movellans, annihilating them as they went. This victory was not achieved without many losses on the human side, and the Draconians were also very much weakened. With the Movellans totally destroyed the humans returned to their own areas of space, hoping to begin a new alliance that could stand against the inevitable return of the Daleks.

Lytton's attack on the prison ship succeeded, and Davros was rescued from his icy tomb. He had been aware throughout those ninety years, and had thought long and hard. He knew that the Daleks had freed him only because he was of use to them—and that they would kill him once he had achieved their purpose. Accordingly, he had no intentions of helping them or placing himself in their power. Rather than leave the station, he insisted on working on it. Using a mind probe, he established control of first the humans assigned to help him, and then two of the Daleks themselves. Davros was forming a loyal core, about which he would create an army that would obey only him.

The Daleks, meanwhile, had hidden their samples of the Movellan virus in the past—the 1980s, in fact, in London. This way, if the containers broke they could not affect any

THE HISTORY OF THE DALEKS

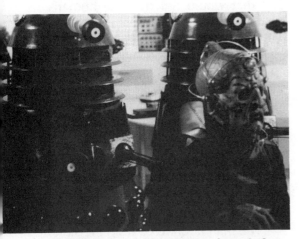

Davros (Terry Malloy) and the Daleks.

Daleks. They allowed the containers to be discovered, then captured the army troops sent in to dispose of them. The Dalek had developed a method of cloning that could duplicate a being, then scan the original's mind, transferring his or her mental patterns to the duplicate. The clone would be loyal to the Daleks and the original would be destroyed. The army troops under Colonel Archer were all treated and left to guard the virus.

Once again, the Doctor and his friends intervened. This time it was the fifth Doctor, along with Turlough and Tegan. The *Tardis* had accidentally impinged on the Dalek time corridor, and the Doctor could not resist investigating this. The Daleks soon detected his presence and arranged for him to be captured. One of their duplicates, Stien, managed the task by winning the Doctor's confidence and then capturing him when they reached the Dalek ship. The Doctor was then prepared for duplication. Knowing that the Time Lords were bound to intervene again in their destiny, the Daleks planned to send a duplicate Doctor to assassinate the High Council of the Time Lords—paving the way for the Daleks to capture all of time. However, the Doctor escaped this fate; the duplication process worked too well and the Doctor was able to access enough of Stien's old self to break the Dalek mind control for a while. Together, they planned to stop the Daleks and kill Davros.

The Daleks had become aware of Davros's treachery, and realized that he would never do as they wished. They had not fooled him any more than he had fooled them. Davros was too dangerous, and the Dalek Supreme ordered him killed. They also planned on exterminating Lytton and his men, who were becoming unreliable allies. The whole plan was crumbling. Davros released the killer virus to stop the Daleks, intending to escape and create a new race for himself—beings programmed with total obedience to his will. The Daleks would obey him in the future, or perish. The Doctor, meanwhile, having again failed to kill Davros, escaped into the past and there released the Movellan virus to destroy the Daleks loyal to Davros.

In both eras the Daleks perished. To his astonishment and fury, Davros discovered that he had enough in common with his Daleks for the virus to affect him also. Meanwhile, Stien had managed to hold together his mental control long enough to destroy the prison station and the accompanying Dalek ship.

On Skaro, the Black Dalek regarded this setback with fury. At least, it seemed, all possible menace from Davros was eliminated. The Dalek scientists evolved a cure for the virus, and the remnants of the Dalek army began to reassemble itself. The way forward was still open.

An excellent opportunity arose when a plague began spreading through the Galaxy. Thanks to their new viral technology, the Daleks were immune to the disease. They soon discovered that most of the humanoid races were not, relying on an elixir to immunize themselves. One essential ingredient for this drug was the mineral Parrinium. This was conveniently located on only one world—the lost planet of Exxilon. No ships that had ever ventured there had ever returned,

but that would not stop the humans and it would not stop the Daleks. Whatever faced them there, they were certain they could overcome it. The plan was for them to obtain what mineral supplies they could and return to Skaro with them. As soon as they left Exxilon, they were to drop a plague bomb on the planet to prevent further expeditions landing there. With the only supply of Parrinium, the Daleks could then negotiate the surrender of worlds for the antidote.

The plan floundered from the start. As the Dalek ship approached Exxilon, a sudden power loss forced it to the ground, where it stayed. Until the source of the drain could be located, they were stranded on the planet. Worse was to come, for the ship was not the only energy source affected by the drain. Emerging from the ship, the Daleks discovered that a human party had beaten them to the planet. They instantly attempted to exterminate, but their guns would not operate; the concentrated power sources used were also now drained. Luckily their lower-powered life-support systems were still working, as they were wired into the Daleks' own mental patterns. It was obvious that the energy drain only worked above a certain minimal level—biological energy was immune and so were low-level explosives.

The Daleks were forced to con-

THE HISTORY OF THE DALEKS

sider the unthinkable: an alliance with the humans until the energy drain could be located and destroyed. Naturally, the Daleks had no intention at all of keeping faith with mere humans. Three Daleks remained hidden in the ship and began developing projectile weapons for armament. Meanwhile, the other Daleks discovered that they must also ally themselves with one of their worst enemies: the third Doctor,

The Exxilons and the Daleks didn't exactly get along too well . . .

and his companion, Sarah Jane. Together, the mixed group headed for the Exxilons but were captured. The primitive armaments of the natives proved effective enough against the humans.

The Exxilons were the descendants of a once great society. They had built a magnificent city, one that would keep itself going forever. It could drain energy from any source to power itself, and it had tendrils that searched through the ground for metals and necessary elements to keep the city in pristine shape. The computer that ran the city rebelled against its creators, throwing them out as impure and unnecessary. Disillusioned and disheartened, the Exxilons for the most part swore off all civilization and descended into barbarism. Few of them retained any semblance of manners or intellect. Instead, the dying race worshipped the city that their forefathers had created centuries earlier.

When the pellet-firing Daleks arrived and began annihilating the Exxilon natives, the Doctor and Sarah escaped into the tunnels beneath the city. Unable to stand against the Daleks, the Exxilons and the humans were forced to surrender. This was exactly what the Daleks needed: a slave work force. All survivors were set to digging Parrinium and storing it in sacks. Meanwhile the Daleks had realized that the city was the source of the energy drain. They opted for a two-pronged attack. Two Daleks were dispatched to enter the city through the tunnels and attempt to destroy the computer. Meanwhile, two of the humans—Galloway and Hamilton—were sent up the side of the city with bombs. On the top of the city was the antenna that received the drained power. They were to destroy this.

Thus far, their planning was impeccable. However, matters began to unravel. Hamilton used his bomb to destroy the beacon on the city, stopping the power drain—and Galloway hid his. He managed to sneak aboard the Dalek ship and hide as the Daleks prepared to leave. Within the city, the Doctor and an Exxilon native, Bellal, teamed to get through the traps that the computer had set. The two Daleks in pursuit managed to solve the problems of the deadly maze. They arrived at the computer center just as it created two zombie figures to fight the Doctor. Recognizing that the Daleks were the greater menace, the computer turned the zombies onto them. The Doctor finished his reprogramming of the computer, ordering it to self-destruct, and he and Bellal were able to escape.

The Daleks were ready to leave, and had the sacks of Parrinium loaded on their ship. They didn't bother to kill

The Doctor (Jon Pertwee) and Bellal (Arnold Yarrow) try to solve the mystery of the Exxilon city.

the humans, knowing that the plague bomb would effect the job for them. As they lifted off, however, Galloway triggered his bomb, destroying the saucer and the remainder of the task force. Sarah and the human female, Jill, had actually substituted sand in

THE HISTORY OF THE DALEKS

the sacks loaded onto the Dalek ship; the Parrinium was now on the human ship, powering up for launch. The humans could cure the plague, and the Dalek plot had been thwarted. The Doctor and Sarah watched the Exillon city melt into nothing, eliminating the energy-drainage problem forever.

Davros was not dead. The virus had only partially affected him, and he had managed to reach an escape pod from the Dalek ship before the explosion. Jetting away from the site, he began to plan his next moves. In this, he proved to be very lucky, for the escape craft came down on Nekros— the world of the living dead.

The whole economy of Nekros was based around the huge fortress of Tranquil Repose. Here the freshly dead were cryogenically preserved and stored to await reawakening in the future, when some cure for what had killed them might be found. Their consciousnesses were kept alive and they were kept informed of what was happening in the Galaxy at large. They were even given a disc jockey to play music for them and alleviate boredom. The problem was that the government did not really wish to bring back the dead. The only ones who could afford Tranquil Repose were those who were very wealthy or politically active, and the politicians knew that reawakening them would result in grave competition for their jobs.

At this juncture, Davros offered a suggestion that was eagerly seized upon. The dead would stay dead, but no one would know. Davros would be established in a laboratory to pretend to cure the fatal illnesses that had killed the sleepers. In fact, he would be making sure they never awoke. In the meantime, the dead could benefit the living in another way: there was a famine in the area and the bodies could be processed to form a protein concentrate to feed the hungry. The government of Nekros agreed to this plan and Davros took over, calling himself the Great Healer. What he had not bothered to tell the greedy political forces on Nekros was that he had his own plans for parts of the undead bodies.

The protein processing worked well, under the control of the ruthless and greedy Kara. She resented paying Davros the money he wanted for his researches, however, and hired Orcini, a Knight of the Grand Order of Oberon, to kill him. Orcini—a somewhat despondent idealist—liked the concept of a quest to kill Davros and undertook the task with his squire, Bostock. Kara was taking no chances, and gave Orcini a bomb that would kill him and Davros the second it was triggered—though she told him it was

Davros (Terry Malloy) is the—ah—head of operations.

merely a signal box. Orcini penetrated the catacombs of Tranquil Repose, where he discovered Davros waiting. Sensing a trap, Orcini killed him—so he throught. But the fake head was only a decoy, and Davros and his Daleks were ready. They slew Bostock.

Davros had been working in secret. Since the Daleks had refused his rule, he had begun to create new Daleks from the bodies in the vaults.

The heads were taken and treated so that they were transformed genetically into Daleks. Davros programmed these Daleks to be completely obedient to him. As soon as he had sufficient funds, he aimed to convert all of the sleeping millions into Daleks, and with his new army wipe out the old Daleks and begin the conquest of the universe. The arrival of Orcini to kill him prompted a slight change of plans, however. The Daleks fetched Kara and confronted her with the evidence of her treachery. Realizing that he had been lied to and tricked, Orcini knifed the greedy woman.

At this point, Davros's final plan matured. He had lured the Doctor to Nekros, determined to finally extract his revenge. This was the sixth Doctor, along with his companion, Peri. There was no way the Doctor could resist such a challenge, and the two old foes were soon face to face again. Davros believed he had all the aces now, but he was wrong. He had neglected the staff of Tranquil Repose, who were annoyed at what he had done to their mausoleums and wanted peace restored. Takis had informed the Dalek Supreme of Davros's hiding place. At Davros's moment of triumph the real Daleks arrived, annihilating Davros's models and capturing their creator.

The Dalek Supreme wanted Dav-

THE HISTORY OF THE DALEKS

ros back on Skaro, for public execution. Cursing and screaming, he was taken off. Takis had hoped that the old order would be restored on Nekros, but the Black Dalek had no intention of that. He would use Tranquil Repose's facilities to continue the Dalek production line—creating Daleks loyal to the Dalek regime, not to Davros. This plan was thwarted by Orcini, who still possessed the bomb that Kara had given him. Triggering the bomb, he destroyed the vaults and the Dalek assembly line, along with himself. He died as he had wished—fulfilling a quest to eradicate evil. The Doctor and Peri suggested to Takis that they use the local plant life to make protein, and thus supply the hungry worlds nearby with food.

The ship carrying Davros had narrowly escaped destruction, having launched into space with moments to spare before Orcini had triggered his bomb. It returned to Skaro with Davros strictly watched at all times. On the Dalek home world, he was brought before the Supreme Council and the Black Dalek for trial. As he had expected, this was mostly a farce played out before the Daleks who watched the events on film. Davros was given the opportunity to speak, the Black Dalek knowing that their crazed creator would never be able to resist.

Davros launched into an impassioned plea to the watching Daleks to swear allegiance to him, and to allow him to lead them to greater victories once agin. He promised to redesign their casings, making them stronger, swifter and more enduring. He promised to oversee their destiny as supreme beings in the universe. Finally the Black Dalek cut him off, and spoke in its turn. Davros had never renounced his claim to be the supreme ruler of the Daleks; to him, they were nothing more than an extension of his own purposes. Instead, the Black Dalek insisted, they could do what was needed without Davros—who would undoubtedly seize his first opportunity to reprogram them to obey him again. Davros could not be trusted; he must be exterminated so that the Dalek race could achieve its own destiny.

Davros called them fools if they rejected him, promising that without him they were doomed. The Daleks refused to listen further, and he was sentenced to death. He managed one last attempt to regain power, for there were some within the Dalek ranks—even within the Supreme Council—who felt that he was possibly telling the truth. At any rate, there were some Daleks who felt that Davros could be used and then discarded once his mind had been drained and utilized.

A rescue attempt was staged but the Black Dalek had been anticipating this. Since the disastrous losses of the Movellan War, he had known that there was talk of overthrowing the Council and reforming the Dalek power scheme. The only reason Davros had been brought to Skaro was to force the rebel elements into the open.

The Black Dalek and his forces struck against the traitors. They succeeded in slaying the dissidents, and this time there was no escape for Davros. The Black Dalek ensured that he was condemned, and he was placed within a matter transmitter. It was set on a broad beam, and his component molecules were scattered about their sun. There would, it seemed, be no way back for Davros this time, despite his rantings and boasts. The war for the final control of the Daleks was over.

For the time being.

Lacking the army they desired, the Daleks alone could not complete their plans for the conquest of the Galaxy. They needed pawns for this task. The Dalek scientists had managed to evolve another variation on time travel—the Time Destructor. This device could locally reverse or accelerate the flow of time. Placed on an enemy world, it could either age the inhabitants to death, or regress the planet millions of years, killing all intelligent forms of life. The Daleks simply had to smuggle one of these devices to each of their enemies' worlds and trigger them.

The problem was that they were powered by a taranium core, and taranium was perhaps the rarest mineral in the Galaxy. A few grams could buy a smallish planet, and a kilo could buy a solar system—if there was a kilo anywhere to be had. The Daleks needed all they could get, and they needed dupes to help them obtain it. Accordingly they plotted a Dalek alliance, offering various alien races the chance to strike at the riches of Earth and the federated space about it. The Daleks were well aware of humanoid greed and stupidity, and—despite the Dalek record—several races joined up with alacrity. Each helped in some aspect of the design and construction of the Time Destructor, though all were unaware of its true aims and powers. The final member of the consortium was perhaps the most unexpected of all—Mavic Chen.

The solar system at this point was at peace. Earth had secured the boundaries of its empire, and, with the good relationship it enjoyed with the Draconians, was safe within its boundaries. The destruction of the Movellans had left both empires in a secure position. The Daleks were ob-

THE HISTORY OF THE DALEKS

viously going to be trouble again, so Earth had formed the SSS—Space Special Security—to check into threats against peace. The SSS was headed by a man named Karlton, under direct command of the Guardian of the Solar System. The Guardian was the elected ruler of Earth and near space—Mavic Chen. Chen, however, had overwhelming ambitions to rule over the entire Terran Empire. Accordingly, he threw his lot in with the Daleks, who promised him (with no intention of paying off) the power he lusted after. Chen in his turn suborned Karlton.

Despite this, Karlton had to follow procedures, and when there were several reports of a Dalek buildup on the planet Kembal, he was forced to dispatch a team of agents to investigate. He simply ensured that the Daleks knew of its arrival, so the mission was bound to fail. Agent Marc Cory discovered that the reports had been correct, and that the Daleks were beginning some plan to invade Earth's empire from Kembal. He also discovered that the Varga plants of Skaro were at large here, and they accounted for his crew. The Varga plants had spines that were doubly poisoned—they induced dementia in humans, then transformed the victims' bodies into Varga plants. Cory discovered much of the plot and recorded the information, but was caught and

killed by the Daleks before he could do anything.

Karlton was forced by procedures to send in a second team, this time Bret Vyon and Kert Gantry. Gantry was killed fairly quickly, but Vyon managed the impossible—he penetrated the Dalek defenses and evaded them long enough to team up with the Doctor, who had once again fortuitously arrived where the Daleks were gathered. This was the first Doctor, and he had with him his companion Steven, and the young girl Katarina, fresh from the battlefields of the Trojan War. The four discovered the details of the Dalek plot, and the Doctor managed to steal the taranium core for the Time Destructor by disguising himself as the cloaked Zephon, the grandly titled Master of the Fifth Galaxy. In the meantime, Vyon, Steven and Katarina managed to power up Mavic Chen's ship, which they used for their escape.

Furious at this setback, the Daleks exterminated Zephon for his stupidity and then used their instruments to cause the ship to crash on the prison world Desperus. Though the Doctor managed to break the ship free of Dalek control, Katarina had to sacrifice her life to keep her friends at liberty. Chen, expecting the fugitives to alert Earth, returned there himself and told Karlton what to expect. The two men laid their plans, convincing the SSS that Vyon had betrayed Earth and was to be killed on sight. From an experimental plant run by Daxter, they received an alert that Vyon had landed there. Karlton dispatched his best agent, Sara Kingdom, to kill Vyon and recover the stolen core. The fact that Sara was Bret Vyon's sister did not prevent her from following what she believed to be her only course of action—killing him. She then went after the Doctor and Steven, but the three of them accidentally stepped into a prototype matter transmitter and recovered on the planet Mira.

Chen was furious at the technicians' mistake, until he realized that Mira was close to Kembal. He alerted the Daleks, pretending this was his planned course of action all along. Sara finally listened to the Doctor and Steven, and realized how she had been tricked. She now threw herself wholeheartedly into helping them. Unfortunately, the planet was the home of the invisible, monstrous Visians, who began hunting the three refugees. Ironically, it was the Daleks who saved them by intruding. The Visians promptly attacked the Dalek party, enabling the Doctor's group to slip away and steal the Dalek ship. The Daleks on Kembal overrode the controls, forcing the ship to land again. On the journey, though, the

Doctor had created a duplicate of the time core. The Daleks didn't dare try to kill the humans, for fear of damaging the precious core. The Doctor knew that the impasse wouldn't last, and agreed to hand it over to them only at the *Tardis*.

Chen forced the Daleks to agree to this and as the exchange took place the Doctor, Steven and Sara managed to reach the safety of the time machine with the real core. The Daleks tested the core and detected the fact that they had been fooled. Once again furious at the delay, they prepared their second time machine and sent it into the Vortex after the *Tardis*. It was another chase through time and space, and the Doctor was again forced to outrun or outwit his greatest foes. After a short stopover at the Lords cricket ground, the two ships materialized on the volcanic world of Tigus. Here the Doctor wished to make his stand but was prevented by the unexpected reappearance of another old foe, the Monk.

The Monk was a Time Lord, like the Doctor. Unlike the Master, he was not evil, but he was certainly irresponsible and derived a great deal of joy from his efforts at altering the course of recorded history. In an attempt to change the outcome of the Battle of Hastings in A.D. 1066 he had run into the Doctor, who stole his demateriali-

THE HISTORY OF THE DALEKS

zation circuit, stranding him in 1066. Having finally made a replacement, the irritated Time Lord was after revenge, in his usual half-brilliant, half-bungling way. He rigged the *Tardis* doors with a special lock to keep the Doctor out—then made the mistake of bragging about it to him. The Doctor broke the lock and entered the *Tardis,* then, unwilling to take on two foes at a time, he set the *Tardis* in motion. This time, both the Daleks and the Monk were on his trail.

The three time machines all appeared within a short time and distance of one another in ancient Egypt.

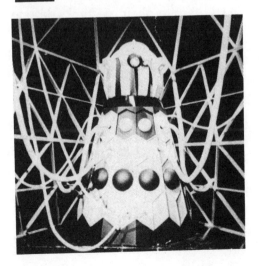

The Emperor Dalek.

Kephren and his men were engaged in building the pyramid of Cheops and did not take kindly to the interference. Chen and the Daleks managed to capture Steven, Sara and the Monk, and would release them only when given the core. The Doctor had no option but to hand it over. Then the Egyptian army arrived before the Daleks could exterminate their prisoners. The Doctor managed to confuse matters somewhat, as the Egyptians and the Daleks engaged in a pitched battle. He took the directional circuit from the Monk's *Tardis*—a more advanced model than his own—and used it to steer his own *Tardis* to Kembal. The Monk was again stranded by the Doctor, but the Daleks and Chen made their escape back to Kembal.

With the taranium core once again in their possession the Daleks had what they really needed, and their allience was dissolved. They locked all their erstwhile allies together, leaving them to ponder their foolishness, while the Time Destructor was prepared. Chen could not accept this final betrayal, and he went crazy. Steven and Sara freed the by-now wiser delegates and allowed them to return to their home worlds and unite those planets with Earth to face the future Dalek onslaught. Chen, however, in his madness, became convinced that the Daleks had misunderstood him.

He captured Sara and Steven and took them to the Daleks, demanding to be placed in command. The Daleks promptly exterminated the maniac.

The Doctor used this diversion to make his way to the Time Destructor, which he set on low power. Instantly everything began to age slowly, and he ordered his companions to make for the *Tardis,* whose internal forces would keep them safe. Steven did as he was told, but Sara stayed to aid the Doctor. As a result she was caught within the advancing field of the Destructor and in moments she aged, withered and finally decayed and turned to dust. The Doctor, being nonhuman, was not as affected, but even he began to feel the effects as he ran for the *Tardis.* Steven helped him the final few feet. In doing so, though, he dropped the Time Destructor, which suddenly went into fast reverse. The Doctor and Steven watched from the *Tardis* control room as everything regressed through time. The Dalek casings eroded away as they passed back before the time of Dalekanium. The creatures themselves died without the protection of the travel machines. Finally all life on Kembal died, and the world was left as arid, shifting sands. The Time Destructor itself ceased to exist.

This threat was gone, but the Daleks were committed to their invasion of the Galaxy. With their allies now turned against them, they found themselves badly outnumbered. The Dalek Wars lingered over the next couple of centuries, but the Daleks were gradually pushed back toward Skaro. It was becoming increasingly obvious that somehow the Daleks were no match for the humanoids they so despised. In fact, for the Daleks even to survive, they needed to adapt themselves.

The experiments by the Dalek Prime on himself were beginning to show fruit. In his attempt to expand his mental capacity, he had grown far larger. He ordered the construction of a specialized life-support system, since he soon lost all mobility. He was becoming pure mentality, and he saw that the future of the Daleks lay in his hands. What he needed was to know why—despite their destiny, despite their power—the Daleks constantly lost their battle to become dominant. He needed answers, and solutions.

He needed the Doctor.

From the very origin of the Daleks down to the end of the Dalek Wars, the ever-changing time traveler had cropped up. At crucial points in their history, the Doctor and his companions had appeared and helped to defeat the Daleks. If anyone knew what it was that made the Daleks vulnerable, it was the Doctor. If anyone could help

THE HISTORY OF THE DALEKS

Victoria (Deborah Watling) and Jamie (Frazer Hines) meet their Dalek captors.

to make the Daleks undefeatable, it had to be the Doctor. The problem was finding a method to ensure his cooperation. From past knowledge, there was no inducement that could win him over—unless it was the possibility of defeating the Daleks forever.

The Emperor Dalek now evolved a plan that was double-layered and devious enough to fool even the Doctor. If the Doctor could be induced to work for the Daleks on the supposition that he was actually helping their defeat, then the plan would succeed. First, though, the Emperor needed a bait on the hook. The obvious place to look was Earth, for the errant Time Lord seemed to love that planet for some odd reason.

Scanning across time, the Daleks discovered that in 1866 two scientists were working on penetrating the time barrier. The Daleks' own ability to travel through time had been dealt a crushing blow with the affair of the Time Destructor, but their surviving equipment was more than sufficient to link up with the feeble efforts of Maxtible and Waterfield on Earth and to form a space-time tunnel from the hills above the Dalek city on Skaro to the country house near Canterbury. The Dalek Supreme passed through, and instantly took control in the past. Both men had daughters, and one—Victoria Waterfield—was taken as a hostage by the Daleks. The Dalek Supreme realized very early on that Maxtible was a greedy man; the Daleks convinced him that they had the power to transmute metals into gold, offering it to him if he would assist them. His alacrity to accept the offer was disgusting to behold, but for the time being he was useful.

The Daleks then took over the house, confining Victoria to one wing. In this wing, they set up recording devices and posted a human to guard the girl. The first phase of their plan was complete. The second was to locate and ensnare the Doctor. Waterfield's time machine was used to penetrate time, until the Doctor or the time field from the *Tardis* was located. They finally discovered a contact in 1966, London. With Victoria a hostage, Waterfield had to play along with the Daleks. Traveling through time, he opened a small antique shop—selling items from his own day! He used the money to hire men to steal the *Tardis* from Heathrow Airport, where the second Doctor had been involved with his companion Jamie, in an affair with alien infiltrators.

Waterfield laid a careful trail back to the store, ensuring that the Doctor would follow it to recover his *Tardis*. The *Tardis* was taken back through time, then transferred to the relay station above the Dalek city on Skaro. As anticipated, the Doctor had little trouble discovering what had happened to his time and space craft, and when he arrived at Waterfield's shop he was trapped with a gas bomb and transported to Maxtible's house, along with Jamie. When they awoke, Waterfield and Maxtible filled them in on what was happening. The Doctor was forced to confront the Daleks.

The Daleks struck a bargain with the Doctor that they knew he couldn't refuse. They informed him that they were seeking the reason they had constantly been defeated in the past, and believed that humans had something in them that Daleks lacked—the human factor. If they could analyze this and duplicate it, then they could instill

the human factor into the Daleks and make them invincible. They carefully did not tell the Doctor that there was a logical flaw in this reasoning, knowing that he would see it and believe that they had overlooked it. If the Daleks were given human attributes, they would know compassion, kindness, pity and affection—which would blunt their power for evil and perhaps turn them into a force for good. This was bound to appeal to the Doctor—and it did. He believed their carefully prepared story, and agreed to aid their research. The chance of turning the destiny of the Daleks around was too great an opportunity to miss.

To get the required readings on the human factor, the Daleks had made the passage to Victoria very difficult. They wanted Jamie to run the gauntlet of their traps so that they could record his honesty, courage, hope, mercy and other human emotions they did not share. Jamie faced the tests well, giving them exactly what they required. But the Daleks were making rather a different use of the data than the Doctor believed. Eventually the Doctor had isolated what he identified as the human factor and instilled it into the computer-augments for the minds of three Daleks. As he had expected, these Daleks became humanized—they started to play with him

THE HISTORY OF THE DALEKS

and Jamie. The Doctor gave them names—Alpha, Beta and Gamma—which was unheard of for the Daleks. These Daleks responded by giving the Doctor a name: Friend.

The Emperor Dalek was pleased with the work done. He dismissed the three Daleks with human factors as of no importance. That had not been the

The Dalek rebellion begins when a Dalek questions the orders of the Emperor.

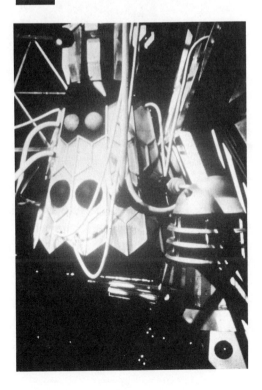

real reason for the project. He issued an order recalling all Daleks to Skaro, and the ones from the house took Victoria with them back to the Dalek city before placing a bomb to destroy that end of the time-space tunnel. The friendly Daleks also returned and the Doctor realized that he must follow, for both Victoria and the *Tardis* were on Skaro. The Emperor had planned all of this, wanting his greatest foe to be on hand at the moment of Dalek triumph. Maxtible plunged through the tunnel, still demanding the secret of transmutation in return for his betrayal of the human race. The Doctor managed to get Maxtible's daughter, Ruth, to evacuate the house; then he, Jamie and Waterfield followed through the tunnel seconds before the bomb detonated.

The humans were captured as soon as they arrived on Skaro, and the Doctor and the Emperor Dalek finally met face-to-face. The Doctor, predictably, was defiant even when defeated. He bravely told the Emperor that the human factor would defeat the Daleks—that the infection would spread. This was sheer bravado, since the Doctor had no idea of the real intentions of the Daleks. The search for the human factor had been simply a smoke screen to keep the Doctor placated. What the Daleks had been after was the Dalek factor—those parts of the Dalek mentality that made them what they were, in contrast to the human factor. The Emperor had no intention of making Daleks more human. On the contrary, with the Dalek factor isolated the plan was to make humans into Daleks.

The Doctor finally realized that he had been outwitted. The Daleks had used him as a pawn and he had fallen for it, in the hope that he could destroy them. In a fit of depression he witnessed the first application of the Dalek factor. The conditioning unit was set up and Maxtible was put through it. He emerged blindly loyal to the Daleks, and willing to do whatever he must. He was a Dalek in all but shape. Pleased with this, the Emperor ordered the Doctor to be used for the next experiment—a fatal mistake. The Dalek factor had been isolated using humans as the base, and the system was set up to work only on humans. The Doctor was far from human, and the conversion process failed to work on him. He pretended, naturally, that it had worked.

Elsewhere in the Dalek city, a supervisor gave an order to a Dalek—and that Dalek questioned the order. This was unheard of, for no Daleks would ever disobey a direct command from a superior. The Doctor knew what it was—the first of the humanized Daleks was exercising his indi-

The Doctor (Patrick Troughton) finally defeated his greatest foes.

viduality and his right to freedom. This was the beginning of a plague that could destroy the rigid structure of Dalek society, and the Emperor was informed immediately. This rot in the heart of Dalek society would have to be eradicated. The problem was that the disobedient Daleks looked exactly like any other Dalek, so how could they be found? The Doctor came up

THE HISTORY OF THE DALEKS

with the obvious answer; the problem was the Daleks with the human factor, so why not order all Daleks to pass through the Dalek-factor conditioning machine? This way the normal Daleks would be unaffected, and the humanized ones would be reversed. The Emperor approved this, and authorized the action.

Since he was faking obedience, the Doctor simply seized his opportunity. He rewired the machine to instill the human factor instead, so that when the Daleks began passing through the machine they were transformed into humanized Daleks. It was a while before this was discovered, and by that point it was too late: Daleks all over the city were questioning orders and refusing to obey. They wanted some say in what was being done, rather than being ordered about by a ridiculous, self-appointed Emperor.

The normal Daleks responded with extermination, and in a matter of minutes civil war broke out. The Doctor used the moment to free his friends and flee the city, which was erupting into an inferno behind him. Waterfield was killed in the escape, and Maxtible met his end in the hills. The Doctor, Jamie and Victoria managed to return safely to the *Tardis*. From this vantage they studied the Dalek city below.

Fighting had intensified, and the city was turning into a war zone. The humanized Daleks broke into the Emperor's control room and proceeded to exterminate the tyrant. With his destruction, the city began to explode. All the Daleks—normal and humanized—perished in the blaze. The last Dalek city collapsed about the remnants of the deadly race. Watching from the hills, the Doctor murmured with satisfaction: "The final end."

The Daleks were no more.

CHAPTER 7

"THE SURVIVORS"

When Terry was asked to submit an outline for his initial story to the *Doctor Who* team, he produced a twenty-six-page rough draft entitled "The Survivors." This was accepted, and eventually became "The Daleks." The original outline contains virtually all of the final plot, but has a few additions and changes that make it an interesting document in its own right. Especially notable is the ending, which is entirely different from the finished version.

The following outline is exactly as he submitted it. It reflects the fact that when Terry was commissioned, the nature of the show was still in flux. Susan at this point was simply another companion, not the Doctor's granddaughter, and the *Tardis* was fully controllable.

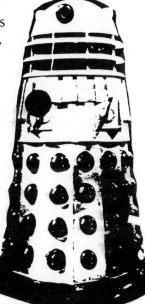

THE SURVIVORS: A STORY LINE FOR THE "DR. WHO" SERIES BY TERRY NATION

The planet is Skaro.

The year, Three thousand.

When Dr. Who and his companions arrive on Skaro, they find it presents a scene of utter desolation. All plant life is in the stage of petrification. The soil is barren. Susan, Barbara and Ian are eager to move on to some other time. Dr. Who, however, is anxious to explore. The dense jungle around them, though now petrified, suggests that the planet was once very fertile. This being so, says Dr. Who, the chances are that animal life existed here. Reluctantly the others agree to a short exploration.

The plant life is all perfectly preserved, but crumbles to dust at a touch. Beautiful flowers dissolve to ash. Trailing vines crack like icicles. As darkness approaches they turn back toward the ship, having seen no sign of life. Dr. Who advances some reason for the death of the planet. Just before the light fails, Ian climbs a small ridge. His shout brings the others to his side. Far below in the valley is a city. Examined through field glasses, it shows no sign or decay, nor does it offer any suggestion of life. They agree that they will go to look at the city the next day, having spent the night in the ship. It is quite dark as they thread through the jungle. Susan sees a very attractive petrified flower and determines to pick it and preserve it in one piece. Her first few attempts shatter the flowers. With great care she tries again. Meanwhile, the others have drawn well ahead of her. Finally Susan succeeds. Then, with the flower cradled in her hands, she becomes aware that someone or something is standing behind her. A hand reaches out and touches her face. With a scream of terror, she runs after the others.

Inside the ship they try to calm her. They suggest the hand was no more than a leaf or a vine brushing against her face. Susan cannot be convinced. They settle down to an uneasy sleep and are awakened by a scratching and a tapping outside the ship. In the darkness they can see nothing of whatever is making the eerie noise. Apart from Dr. Who, all are convinced that they

"THE SURVIVORS"

should leave Skaro at once. Dr. Who argues that they must try to contact whatever life remains on the planet, and discover what caused its destruction. There is a general ganging-up against Dr. Who, who becomes very stubborn. Ian and Barbara preach at him about democratic rights and the wishes of the majority. Eventually, Dr. Who appears to capitulate. He moves to the controls and fiddles for a moment, then attempts to start the ship. It fails, as do further attempts. He strips an instrument and says he has found the fault. A leak in a liquid fuse. He baffles the others with a flow of technical jargon, coming finally to the fact that the fuse has to be refilled with fluid. Water would do, he says. Ian points out that there is no water in the ship, and they have seen no sign of any in the jungle. Barbara plays into Dr. Who's hands when she suggests that there *must* be water in the city. During the rest of that sleepless night, no more tapping is heard. At first light, they emerge cautiously from the ship. There is no sign of the things they heard outside, until Susan finds a small metal container near the side of the ship. They presume it has been dropped by one of the marauders. They open it and find it contains glass phials of what appears to be a drug. They stow it safely in the ship and start out for the city.

The journey is uneventful, and they find the city fascinating. The streets are roofed. The shops are filled with foodstuffs that crumble at a touch. The buildings are more modern than those they knew on Earth, glass being widely used in design. Everything is intact and undamaged. The floors and roadways are made from a metal material. There are no steps anywhere, only sloping ramps. Dr. Who is excited. They make their headquarters in what appears to be a public building. Dr. Who directs each of them to go in a different direction, and find, if they can, books, or whatever replaced books. Dr. Who hopes to learn something of the history of the planet. Ian reminds them that they have come here to find water. Dr. Who agrees testily. They arrange to meet back at the starting point in an hour. We follow each of them, and see something of their discoveries. One by one they return to the meeting place. First Susan and Ian, then Dr. Who, but no sign of Barbara.

Barbara is wandering through a hall of strange sculptures. As she walks, we see a lens in a wall turn to follow her movements. She walks down a corridor. As she turns out of sight, a door slides shut behind her.

Outside, Dr. Who's party is growing more anxious.

Barbara panics slightly, as more

and more corridors seem to lead to dead ends.

Ian decides they must start to search for Barbara.

Fear grows in Barbara when she turns back along a passage down which she has just come and finds it blocked off. She starts to run. Outside the searchers enter a building calling Barbara's name. She hears nothing as she runs into another blank wall. In a frenzy of temper and fear she pounds at the wall. Sobbing, she gives up and turns to return the way she has come, and finds to her horror that she is in a room. Four blank walls, with no indication of where she entered. She hears a slight whir of machinery, lurches slightly and the room begins to sink.

Her three companions are wandering through a building calling her name when Ian silences them. Far away they hear an irregular ticking sound. They follow the sound and enter a room filled with scientific instruments. The ticking emanates from one of these. Ian identifies it as a type of geiger counter. The needle is resting in a section of the dial marked Danger. Dr. Who now realizes what has happened on Skaro. It has been destroyed by an atomic war. Ian asks how the city could have survived, and they conclude that the attack was made with neutron bombs, a weapon

that destroys tissue but not solid matter. Kills the people and preserves the buildings. What is more to the point is that they have been exposed to a high level of radiation. Dr. Who admits to feeling unwell.

Barbara feels a slight jolt, and the whirring noise stops. A door slides open in front of her, revealing a passage. She starts cautiously along it. She reaches a fork in the corridor and hesitates while deciding which to follow. Behind her, a panel opens and a pair of grotesque arms move out to encircle her.

Above ground, Ian insists that Dr. Who return to the ship and take it to a period where Susan and the doctor can be treated for radiation. Susan points out that the ship is out of action. Sheepishly Dr. Who shows them the liquid fuse which is in perfect condition. Ian suspected as much. However, this is no time for recriminations. Ian says he will stay and search for Barbara while Dr. Who and Susan return to the ship. Reluctantly they agree. Ian goes with them to the doorway of the building. As they turn to leave they are confronted by four terrifying machine-like creatures. Ian tries to run for it. A weapon is pointed at him and his legs crumple, temporarily paralyzed.

Barbara is seated on the floor of a windowless room, sobbing, when she

"THE SURVIVORS"

hears sounds outside. A moment later Ian, Susan and the Doctor are hustled in and the door closed again. Like her, they have been searched and belongings have been taken from them. Other than that they are unharmed. Barbara tells them she is feeling unwell, and they explain to her about the radiation. Unless they get treatment soon, there is little hope. Dr. Who is taken away to be questioned by the leaders of the underground city. On the way, he notices a gigantic control room and hears the sound of thundering water. He learns that the people of the underground city are the Daleks, the descendants of the survivors of a Neutron War two thousand years before. The city below ground was prepared before the war to ensure the survival of a select group. The war was started by the people of the other hemisphere—the Thals. The Thals had depended for survival not on a vast underground shelter, but on an antiradiation drug they had developed. This fact rings a bell for Dr. Who and he remembers the phials found outside the ship. The Daleks have always believed the Thals to be extinct. Until now that is, for they presume that Dr. Who and his companions are Thals. He inquires about their fate and is told that they are to be tried for the crimes of their forefathers against the Dalek people. Revenge still runs strong in the Daleks, and even after two thousand years, they intend to punish the Thal people for the crime of starting the war.

The trial is to take place after the great rain. Dr. Who learns that each decade there is a great rain on Skaro. After each the radiation level drops sharply. After this rain, it should be low enough for the Daleks to start life above ground again. It would be propitious therefore, if their emergence were marked by the execution of the Thals.

Dr. Who points out that unless they receive treatment quickly, they will not survive until the rain is finished. He begs that one of them be allowed to return to the ship to fetch the drugs, hoping against hope that the phials are indeed the antiradiation preparation that they need. Dr. Who

is told that the matter will be considered, and is returned to the cell.

They are all feeling the effects of the radiation poisoning when later that night, a Dalek comes to their room and tells them it has been agreed that one of them can go for the drugs, and that the child has been selected. Although frightened of the jungle and what it might hold, Susan is determined to go despite the protestations and pleas that one of the adults be allowed to go. Eventually, Susan sets out.

The thunder and lightning that precede the great rain make her journey through the stone jungle the more terrifying. She reaches the ship unmolested. Inside, she treats herself with the drug, and packing it up, prepares for the return journey. She is about to start when she hears the same eerie tapping as before.

Back in the cell the others are concerned for Susan. There is some abuse of Dr. Who for letting them in for this. They try to evolve an escape plan, but know that they would not be strong enough to carry it out.

Susan, very afraid, knows that time is running out. Outside the tapping continues. Taking her courage in one hand and a large spanner in the other, she steps outside.

A half-circle of figures stands back in the shadows, lit sometimes by the flickering lightning. Susan calls out

"THE SURVIVORS"

and asks who they are. The answer comes back in a gentle human voice. They are what remains of the Thals. Always keeping in the shadow, the spokesman tells her that there are now fewer than one hundred of them. The antiradiation drug was not powerful enough to counter the intense radiation of the first thousand years after the war. Those who did survive produced mutations. Eventually, these mutations settled into a genetic pattern, and the race has become uniform. They are still ashamed of their malformed bodies. Susan moves closer, and in a sustained flash sees them, fully. They are identical to the human race on Earth, but perhaps even more beautiful. She learns that they have lived from the vast stockpiles of food that were prepared before the war. Now these stocks have almost run out. They need help if they are to survive, and the only people who can help them are the Daleks. The Thals tell her that it was not they who started the war, but the Daleks. Susan says she will tell the Daleks of their plight, and now she must return to the city with the drugs. She learns that the drugs were left by intent, the Thals knowing that the radiation would affect them. As the rain starts, they give her a cape. They escort her to the outskirts of the city, and leave her saying that if the Daleks wish to help, they can leave a message outside the city gates.

Susan reaches the cell and administers the drug. She tells the others that she was questioned on her return by the Daleks, and told them of her meeting with the Thals. Later that day, a Dalek visits them and says a message has been sent to the Thals inviting them to come to the city and collect food when the rain has ended. Susan is not so pleased when the Dalek adds that not only will food be waiting, but guns. They intend to eliminate the Thals from the face of the planet, and ensure, he says, that no war will ever happen again.

The time travelers are recovering quickly, and realize that they must warn the Thals of the treachery. They plot to escape. Dr. Who is convinced that the suits worn by the Daleks are powered by electricity drawn up through the metal floor. The "eye" of the suit is a television lens on a flexible shaft. The suit has no legs, the base being mechanized for movement. Ian points out that the Dalek that brings their food never actually enters their cell. First, then, they must lure him in, then immobilize him. As the plan develops, Ian notices the plastic cape that the Thals gave Susan when the rain started. This he takes from her, and to her surprise, tells her to scrape the mud from her shoes. He directs the others to do the same, then he starts to explain his plan.

When the Dalek brings their food, Susan is sitting on the floor near the opening of the door. The moment it starts to slide open she slips a small piece of metal (taken from the drug box) into the runner. The Dalek orders them to take the food, which they do. The plastic cape is laid on the floor near the door. The Dalek pushes the control outside the cell and the door starts to slide shut. It clicks violently as it balks against the metal in the runner. The Dalek tries the switch again with the same result. He opens the door again, and his flexible eye moves down to the runner. This is the cue for action. Barbara, who has been kneading the mud from their shoes into a muddy paste, slaps it over the lens with a splosh, blinding the creature. At the same instant, Ian and Dr. Who grab its sides and pull it forward. It struggles violently and throws them off, and unseeingly lurches forward onto the plastic cape. This insulates the machine from its power source and it becomes helpless. Ian moves quickly to open the machine. He is revolted by the creature he finds inside, and tells the two girls to look away. With the aid of Dr. Who, the creature, helpless out of its machine, is pushed in a corner. With difficulty, Ian climbs into the machine suit. Then, with the

others ahead of him, they start out of the cell along the corridor. We get a glimpse of the frog-like animal that is a Dalek as it lies, unable to move, in the cell.

Susan leads the way, remembering the path she was taken before she went back to the ship. Outside a formidable steel door is a Dalek on guard. Ian speaks to him, imitating the strange metallic voice of the Daleks. He says that the prisoners have to be taken up to the fourth level. The guard doesn't doubt him, and the doors slide open. The prisoners move inside. There is a lift at one side of this chamber. The door slides shut and Dr. Who slams home some bolts. Ian tries to free himself from inside the suit, but one of the interior locking nuts has twisted tight. At that moment, they hear alarm bells starting to sound. Ian screams at the others to get in the lift. They try to help him, but he pushes them toward it. He will not allow them to stay with him, and the suit is too bulky to allow them all into the lift at the same time. He forces them in, and starts the control for the top. As the lift vanishes upward, there is a hammering on the door. Ian struggles to free himself. A voice outside orders that the cutters be used. Slowly an arc of molten metal appears on the door as they cut into it. The others in the lift

"THE SURVIVORS"

reach the surface and quickly send the lift back down. They watch the indicator needle.

Below, the door is almost cut through. It falls with a crash and we see, from the Daleks' viewpoint, Ian's stolen suit in the middle of the chamber. Instantly it is fired on with heat guns, and the suit bursts into flame. The Daleks enter and approach the suit cautiously. Then we discover that it is empty. The lift indicator is nearing the top. A Dalek speeds toward the controls to halt it.

Above ground, the open-fronted lift is just appearing, much to the joy of the others, but before it can reach full ground level, the Dalek reaches the control and it starts to descend. Ian is dragged from the lift with inches to spare.

There is still no time to waste, as the rain has stopped, and the Thals are heading for an ambush. Cautiously the escapers make their way through the building. They see the food piled on the floor, and hiding around, armed Daleks. They scream a warning to the Thals as the first of them appears in the doorway. In the resulting confusion, they make their escape, and join the Thals at the ship in the jungle. At this meeting, Dr. Who and the others learn something more of the Thal people. They are dedicated to end killing,

and even if it means their extinction, they are determined that they will not attack the Daleks. Ian tries to fire them with the desire for survival, but they explain that the race memory of such a cataclysmic war has erased all instinct to fight. The Thals tell them to go on their way. This is not their problem. With really no alternative, the time travelers agree. They move back to the ship, when suddenly Dr. Who remembers. The liquid fuse. It was taken from him by the Daleks when he was searched, and now lies in the city from which they have just escaped.

Now, reasons Ian, their problem is the same as the Thals'. They must join forces if they are to survive, and to survive, they must get back into the city. The Thals agree on the condition that there is no killing. These people are not lacking in courage or compassion.

They start to plan. Dr. Who believes that the whole city is powered from the central control room he saw during their captivity. The power for the lifts, the movement machines, the air intakes, in fact everything that makes the city work is centered in that room. This, says Dr. Who, is the brain of the city.

Ian expounds the theory that the most vulnerable area to attack is the one considered by the defenders to be the most invulnerable.

They consider the lifts and the air intakes, but suspect that these will be heavily guarded. Dr. Who asks the source of the water he heard in the city. This comes, he is told, from the lake behind the mountain that backs the city, but there is no hope of reaching the city from that area. It is invulnerable. Then that must be where they attack, says Ian. The Thals are horrified. The lake, they say, is filled with frightful marine life mutated into monsters. They will face dangers not only from the Daleks but also from the amphibian creatures that swarm the swamps around the lake. Even more reason for making this the area of their attack, says Ian. The Daleks will never expect an attack from this area.

The Thals are not convinced, as they are certain there is no access to the city this way. However, they will go along. Dr. Who is in favor of taking a large force, but Ian opposes this, maintaining that a small mobile force can work more effectively. After more discussion it is agreed that Ian will head this force, taking six Thal men with him. Susan, Barbara and the Doctor will remain near the city, with the rest of the Thals. Ian sets a date by which, if he is going to succeed, he will be ready to move into the city. Dr. Who must mount a diversionary attack on that date.

Ian's group prepares to move out when Barbara joins him. She insists on being in on this, and no amount of protesting will change her mind. Her motives would be hard to define. Ian's welfare? Love of adventure? Or the very good-looking Thal going with them? They set off, and Dr. Who settles down to wait and study the old books and records of the Thals.

The swamp that borders the lake is as dangerous and uncomfortable as the Thals predicted. A land of mist. The camp beside the lake frightens Barbara beyond words. The terrible sounds of the marine creatures. Leeches like octopuses that seem to lurk in every pool. Any attempt to sleep is wasted. A Thal who goes down to the water's edge at dawn is remembered only by the scream he leaves behind.

In daylight, Ian examines the cliff face that walls one end of the lake. The tunnels that take the water into the underground city are fractionally below the surface of the flooded lake. The water rushes down the tunnels with great force, and it is obvious that no entry can be made that way. Above the water line, Ian can see a honeycomb of caves and fissures. He decides to explore these in the hope that they will lead deep into the mountain, and perhaps into the city. A difficult and dangerous traverse along the cliff face is necessary to reach them. To fall

"THE SURVIVORS"

into the lake below would mean certain death, for the water writhes with black, shapeless creatures.

The first few caves they examine end ten or twenty feet beyond their entrances. Ian is losing hope when a Thal reports a cave that seems to go much deeper. This is the route they select, and they start their journey into the mountain.

At the ship, meanwhile, Dr. Who continues his studies of the prewar civilization.

The equipment carried by the party in the mountain is hardly suitable for so arduous a journey. A flashlight from the ship. Some candles and ropes made by the Thals. Ian is tempted to give up the attempt, but soon after the start, he is robbed of the choice by a landslide that blocks their retreat. As they move deeper into the mountain, the heat starts to build, making the journey more uncomfortable. They edge along chasms that seem bottomless. At one point, Barbara is left to rest while the others go off in different directions to seek a route. In the darkness beyond the weak light of her candle, she hears a slithering sound, and her own childhood nightmare is fulfilled when she sees the giant spiders, white and bloated, starting toward her.

Later, a Thal sacrifices himself by cutting a rope from which he hangs

after a fall, and which threatens the lives of the others.

A candle ignites a jet of natural gas, and its flame blazes intermittently across their path. A quick dash across its path as it subsides is the only way to pass, and there is no way to estimate its timing. An error, and the passer could be caught in the inferno.

Every hundred yards provides a new terror, and the group faces these perils with no certainty that they will ever escape. Time is now against them as the moment for Dr. Who's diversionary attack grows near.

When all hope is lost, Ian makes one last exploration. He finds a narrow fissure through which he can hear the sound of water. The party creeps through and emerges into a great chamber where the water from the lake rushes through. Here, they find stonework that channels the water and they know they are near the city.

Dr. Who prepares his attack. He plans to block off some of the air vents if he can, and generally make things uncomfortable for the Daleks.

From the mountain, Ian and Barbara's group enters the city.

Dr. Who, in his enthusiasm, gets captured by the Daleks with Susan and a few Thals.

Ian's party meanwhile is making good progress.

The Daleks do not intend to be

cheated of their execution again, and Dr. Who and his group are taken to the sonic chamber, the Daleks' particular form of capital punishment. The victims are subjected to a rising level of decibels that become ultrasonic, driving them through madness to death. With particular venom, the Daleks prolong the agony as much as possible.

Ian's attack is helped by the attention the execution is getting, and they are able to move forward with not too much difficulty. The final phase of the battle is entered when they reach the central control room. Here they are opposed most strongly.

Outside the sonic chamber, the Daleks watch the growing agony of their victims. The Dalek at the control lever moves it toward the peak. Dr. Who and the others in the chamber are reaching the limit of endurance when the sound stops. The Dalek travel machines become lifeless. The lights fail. Ian has succeeded.

The vanquished Daleks are being treated with compassion by the Thals. Discussions are held to find a way by which both races can survive in peace. The Thals mistrust the Daleks, rightly, as is proved later. During this time, Dr. Who studies the records of the Daleks, and compares them with his earlier study of Thal records.

A Dalek reports seeing two unaccountable blips on the space radar. This is given little attention. Using the freedom given them by the Thals, the Daleks launch a counterattack on the control room. Dr. Who halts the battle with the announcement that he has discovered from the records that neither the Thals nor the Daleks were to blame for the war. Both hemispheres were destroyed simultaneously, and there is evidence that before the attack the radar had recorded something in space. Now again the planet is being approached by an unknown force. The prospect of attack from an outside agent provides the best possible unifying motive for the Thals and the Daleks. Together they prepare to meet the new invaders, knowing that if they survive, they can coexist on their planet.

Jointly they plan their defense as the rockets move closer to the planet.

Dr. Who's party, having recovered the vital liquid fuse, can now leave when it wants. When Dr. Who suggests this to his companions, the idea is rejected violently. They have been through a great deal, and intend to see this through.

The rockets land, and the invaders advance on the city. A group of Dalek skirmishers fire on the attackers, and find their weapons have no effect whatever. The space people seem to be protected by an invisible shield.

"THE SURVIVORS"

They appear to be invulnerable. It is Dr. Who who realizes that the invaders, despite the most violent aggression from the Daleks, have not returned the fire. Despite the fears of the others, Dr. Who advances on the invaders unarmed and attempts to make contact. Carefully the space people emerge, and Skaro learns the final truth.

These people come from the planet that two thousand years earlier fired neutron bombs on Skaro. Since that time, their own civilization has progressed and they have realized the enormity of the crime committed by their forefathers. They have waited for the radiation level to fall, and now they come to make reparations and assist in rebuilding the planet.

With Skaro's safe future assured, Dr. Who and the others leave for new times and distance.

CHAPTER
8

"THE DESTROYERS"

Over the years, only one Dalek script has never been filmed —the projected pilot episode for the American television series. It was to run for thirty minutes, with a teaser and a midstory commercial break. What follows is a breakdown of the plot for that tale: "The Destroyers."

Carson and Wayne are members of a space exploration team. They are guarding their base dome, surrounded by a force field. Despite this, the Daleks penetrate the field, killing Carson. His death alerts Wayne, Morgan

and Sara Kingdom. Sara sounds the alarm, and the base errupts into violence as the Daleks attack. There are apparently no survivors.

The SSS sends in three agents to investigate. They are Captain Jason Corey, David Kingdom (Sara's brother) and Mark Seven. Mark is in fact an android, stronger and more logical than any human being, with pedantic speech patterns.* They discover Whitman still alive. He cannot identify their attackers but tells them that they

* This story was written three years before *Star Trek* appeared in England. Mark Seven, though similar to Spock, is of a different origin. He is an android, not alien/human.

took a few prisoners; he then expires. Sara is in fact alive also, but wounded and dodging the Daleks in the jungle. The Daleks have Philip Leigh as a prisoner for interrogation. Their instrumentation detects movement at the dome, and they send a patrol out to annihilate whatever is alive there. The agents have discovered the Dalek tracks and are following them when the Daleks approach the dome. Jason, Mark and David hide in the bushes, where they are attacked by man-eating plants.

Mark makes a noise, and the Daleks blast away at the bushes before proceeding on their way to the dome. Jason and David now free themselves with their knives and go to Mark's aid. Being a robot, he is mostly undamaged from the attack, and needs only minor repairs before he is functional again. Sara has taken refuge by accident in the cave that houses the entrance to the Daleks' underground base. They activate their defense mechanisms, shadowy spectres that attack her, enveloping her in webbing. When she is helpless, the Daleks take her captive.

Jason, David and Mark find the cave, just ahead of the Dalek patrol returning from the dome. Their way forward is blocked by a chasm, but knowing there must be some way for the Daleks to cross it they hide, and see two Daleks activate a tubular bridge. As one crosses they jump the other, and Mark tosses it into the chasm. The first Dalek tries to return but David deactivates the bridge, sending the creature plunging into the abyss. In Dalek central control, Leigh is eliminated now that they have a better prisoner in Sara. The Black Dalek orders the ship prepared for departure. The agents arrive at the perimeter in time to see this, but not in time to stop it. The Dalek ship launches, taking Sarah with it.

The invasion of Earth is beginning.

CHAPTER 9

THE DALEK BOOKS AND RECORDS

Over the past twenty-five years, a number of books featuring the Daleks have appeared. Excluding those based on the television stories (all published by W.H. Allen/Target Books), these include:

The Dalek Book (Souvenier Press, 1964), written by David Whitaker and Terry Nation. This included stories, comics and even a Dalek dictionary. A special photographic insert about the first movie was also featured. Both this and the next book contained stories set in the Universe of the SSS and Mark Seven.

The Dalek Outer Space Book (Souvenier Press, 1965), written by David Whitaker and Terry Nation. This contained similar material, plus a photographic section telling a story of Susan meeting the Daleks. These were actually reworked stills from the first Dalek television adventure.

The Dalek Pocketbook and Space Travellers Guide (Panther Books, 1965). This was a half-and-half mixture of fiction and fact. The first section, about the Daleks, was written by Terry Nation. The second section was a general guide to astronomy.

The Doctor Who and the Daleks Omnibus (St. Michaels, 1976). This was edited by Terry Nation, with a few articles and photos from the TV show. Also included were illustrated versions of the Target novels "Genesis of the Daleks" and "The Planet of the Daleks" written by Terrance Dicks.

Terry Nation's Dalek Annual (World Distributors). Four Christmas annuals were released, dated 1976–1979. Each contained stories and picture strips, some of them reprints of the old *TV21* strips. The stories were about the "Anti-Dalek Force," a sequel to Terry's SSS. Mark Seven (from "The Destructors" pilot) was also included.

▶ Records

Daleks were equally popular on records. Apart from the Century 21 recording of "The Chase" (see the notes on that story for further details) and the soundtrack recording taken from "Genesis of the Daleks," other records included:

"Dance of the Daleks," by Jack Dorsey and His Orchestra (Polydor, 1965)

"The Eccentric Dr. Who/Daleks and Thals," by the Malcolm Lockyer Orchestra (Columbia, 1965)

"All I Want for Christmas Is a Dalek," by the Go-Jos (written by Johnny Worth). This featured a photo cover, with the studio group looking at a picture of a Dalek.

"Landing of the Daleks," by the Earthlings (1965). This had the distinction of actually being banned from being played on the radio—not because of offensive lyrics, but because the track began with the morse code for SOS. The BBC wouldn't play it, but Radio Luxembourg did. Luxembourg's transmitters were working on a frequency close to that of ships and coastal radio stations, and consequently the record was heard several times and assumed to be from a ship in distress. Luxembourg then agreed not to play the record again.

CHAPTER
10

THE
DALEKS ON
EXHIBITION

As the Daleks became popular, the commercial aspects of having them on display for the public (mostly children) became obvious. Their first public appearance was at the then-annual "Daily Mail Boys and Girls Exhibition" at the Empire Hall, Olympia, during the Christmas 1964 season. Two Daleks were there, the Black Dalek and one of the regulars from "The Dalek Invasion of Earth" television story. Children rode through the exhibition on a train while the Daleks moved about and chanted their battle-cry, "Exterminate!" Carole Ann Ford (who played the original companion,

Susan) was even there, on December 28, in person. She had a heavy schedule that Christmas going around stores signing copies of *The Dalek Book*.

The Daleks were to return to Empire Hall three years later during Christmas 1967. This time around, they were joined by other monsters, like the Cybermen and Yeti. Also present were two more of Terry's creations, the Mire Beast and the Fungoid, both from "The Chase."

On December 21, 1971, two Daleks appeared at (logically enough) a Young Observer show in the London Planetarium. This was part of a special show hosted by companion Peter

DOCTOR WHO AND THE DALEKS

The Doctor (Jon Pertwee) meets the Daleks—at the Science Museum in London.

Purves, and featuring Jon Pertwee and producer Barry Letts.

In March and April 1972, there was a special display in the Ceylon Tea Centre in London to show the entries for the BBC's official "Win a Dalek" competition.

The year 1973 saw a longer-running exhibition in the Science Mu-seum in Kensington, London, as a part of a "BBC TV Special Effects Exhibition." Two Daleks built for the show were present, again moving slightly and "talking." This showed the BBC that there was a tremendous interest on the part of the public in a Doctor Who exhibition, and the following Easter two of them appeared. The one

THE DALEKS ON EXHIBITION

at Longleat House is still going (indeed, a special twentieth-anniversary convention there drew crowds of thousands). The second, on Blackpool's Golden Mile, closed in 1985. Both exhibitions prominently featured the Daleks, with looped-tape dialogue. Their name was displayed outside of the Blackpool Exhibition, along with that of the show.

The Doctor Who *Exhibition in Blackpool featured the Daleks very strongly.* © *JOHN PEEL*

THE DALEK COMIC STRIPS

The first comic strip to feature the Daleks was also without doubt the best. Gerry Anderson's Century 21 Productions had inaugurated a TV-oriented comic featuring mostly his own shows—*TV21*. There were also strips based on other series, including *The Munsters, My Favorite Martian,* and *Burke's Law.* The comic was issued weekly, with color covers and inserts. It was designed as a newspaper with the cover date one hundred years in the future from the actual date. The back cover for the first two years (there were 104 issues in all) featured "The Daleks," beginning January 23, 1965.

The strip was immensely popular; it told how the Daleks came to be created, all about their wars with the Mechonoids, and finally how they discovered Earth. This was all a prologue to the TV story "The Dalek Invasion of Earth," and at this point the strip ended. The comic had some interesting points, notably a completely different version of the creation of the Daleks. In the story, the Daleks were large headed and blue skinned, and they built a neutron bomb to destroy the Thals. Their war leader, Zolfian, prepared for battle, but a meteorite storm impacted on the factory and set off the neutron bomb. The planet

WIN A REAL DALEK!!

TV CENTURY 21

ADVENTURE IN THE 21st CENTURY

7D

No. 28 UNIVERSE EDITION   EVERY WEDNESDAY   DATELINE: July 31, 2065

DR. WHO and the DALEKS

Peter Cushing and Roberta Tovey are captured by the Daleks.

PEACEFUL THALS AMBUSHED!

DALEKS! DALEKS! TO BE WON!

"FOLLOWING attempts to make peace with the Daleks, the Thals have been viciously ambushed and a fierce battle is still being fought."

This was the first frightening news of the Daleks to hit the Universe some eighteen months ago on B.B.C. Television.

Now the exciting film, "Dr. Who and the Daleks" is on the cinema screen in glorious Technicolour. You can see it at your local cinema soon.

SOLTURIAN NEWS AGENCY FLASH:—

Prince Jareth has been called in by Mirva to investigate another prophesy of Lurr. It is still not certain whether Lurr is continuing his opposition to the Daleks, or whether this new look into the future is concerned with other events.

(Full story page 20)

CORGI MODEL CLUB NEWS — EVERY WEEK PAGE 19

STOP PRESS

LONDON ANT BATTLE

Reports are coming in of fierce street fighting in the streets of London as European troops struggle to overcome massed armies of giant ants.

GHOST GALLEON SIGHTED !

Excited radio message from Lt. Phones Sheridan of the W. A. S. P. vessel Stingray reports sighting a ghostly galleon nearing tracking station 17.

ACTOR SHOT

Actor 'Lord' Nelson was shot on the stage of the theatre during a performance of the play 'This Gun for Death'.
Captain Amos Burke is investigating.

TV21 #46

was virtually destroyed, but Zolfian and his chief scientist, Yarvelling, survived.

They roamed Skaro, searching for survivors, with no luck. Finally, they were discovered by the first of the Daleks. Yarvelling had built a machine to be a mobile killing device. The Daleks that survived the war were hideously mutated and used these machines to live and move about. The two old Daleks lived long enough to begin production of the Dalek machines and to make the first of the new Daleks a special casing, in gold. He was the Emperor Dalek.

To create the effect in print of the grating Dalek speech, the strip cleverly used squared-off lettering. This distinctive script stood out well. One of the comic's artists was Chris Achilleos, who would later do the earliest Target Book covers for the Doctor Who novels. The strip was fast-paced and extremely well drawn, despite the initial problem that the Dalek machines were shown with a nonexistant grating next to their arms and guns; this was a misunderstanding. (See the Behind the Scenes note on "The Daleks" TV adventure for details.)

With the end of this strip, the Daleks were featured from time to time in the "Doctor Who" strip itself. This had begun in *TV Comic*, another tie-in to many shows, with the issue of

Dr Who Weekly #17

November 14, 1964. On January 21, 1967—one week after the end of "The Daleks" in *TV21*—the strip in *TV Comic* became "Doctor Who and the Daleks." This lasted for six months, until Terry made his decision to withdraw the Daleks from the BBC and attempt to sell the idea as a series

THE DALEK COMIC STRIPS

in the U.S. They would not return for several years to the comics. The "Doctor Who" strip was switched to a new magazine called *Countdown* in 1971, later retitled *TV Action.* The Daleks appeared in several stories under this format.

With the demise of *TV Action,* the "Doctor Who" strip reverted to *TV Comic* again on September 1, 1973.

When Jon Pertwee regenerated to Tom Baker, there were again a few stories that featured the Doctor fighting the Daleks. Finally, on October 17, 1979, the first issue of *Doctor Who Weekly* was launched. Prominent on the cover, naturally, was a Dalek. The first issue saw them in a story of their own, without the Doctor: "The Return of the Daleks." Then, in issue 17, they

Dr Who *(Marvel Comic)*

were given a foe of their own to fight: "Abslom Daak, Dalek Killer." Daak proved popular and returned several times to fight the Daleks. On May 7, 1980, the Doctor and the Daleks finally faced off for a fight. Then, beginning with issue 33, the old Dalek strip from *TV21* was reprinted. This ran until issue 42, reprinting forty-four of the old strips. In issue 53 the strip returned, and with issue 56 it went to color as the back-cover feature. Skipping an occasional issue, it ran for another eleven installments, making a total of sixty-seven of the original one hundred four pages reprinted.

The *Doctor Who Weekly* had become first *Doctor Who Monthly,* then *Doctor Who Magazine.* It was published by the English arm of Marvel Comics. With the growing popularity of the show in the U.S., a monthly Marvel comic was published here from October 1984 to August 1986— twenty-three issues in all. It was basically simply a colorized reprint of the English strips, and the Daleks were once again prominently featured. Issue 4 featured the comic's only wraparound cover, and—hardly surprisingly—the Daleks were the main subject once again!

AFTERWORD

This book contains all of the known facts about the Daleks, but writing a definitive history of them at this stage is probably impossible. Though the general impression of history is that it is a static recital of dates and events, of kings, battles and plagues, it is not that simple. When everything looks as though it has been nailed down and pinned to a historical timetable, along will come some new fact and overturn accepted versions. No one believed that Troy was real until a dreamer discovered its remains. Howard Carter's discovery of the tomb of Tutankhamen was an unexpected success in an area previously thought to have been mined dry.

The same may yet happen with the Daleks. The history of that xenophobic race as chronicled here is completely accurate—and yet who is to say that some day soon, another new chunk of their story might not come to light? It seems more than likely that this will be the case. Throughout the twenty-five years *Doctor Who* has been on the air, the Daleks have been an integral part of the story. If there is one thing that you can be certain of, it is that if *Doctor Who* lasts another twenty-five years, then the Daleks will be facing him again. We may know their origin and their eventual end, but there are still undoubtedly many tales untold of their lives and battles.

Depend upon it: the Daleks will return!

APPENDIX

▶ Addresses

If, after reading this book, you're interested in learning more about Doctor Who and the Daleks, or in joining a fan club, or in purchasing photographs, then the following people are recommended.

NOTE!!: for all overseas addresses, be certain to enclose *two* international reply coupons, along with a self-addressed envelope.

▶ In-Vision

This is simply the very best magazine available on the Tom Baker years of the show. Each monthly release is twelve pages long, has a color cover, and many interior photographs. The releases deal with a single story at a time; they contain interviews, behind-the-scenes accounts, reviews, and complete cast and credit listings.

Jeremy Bentham
13 Northfield Road
Borehamwood
Hertfordshire
WD6 4AE
England

▶ The Friends of Doctor Who

This is a fan club run by Lionheart Television International, the American arm of the BBC. Its dues are five dollars per year, which includes a quarterly newspaper and membership kit. Various merchandising items are also offered.

The Friends of Doctor Who
Lionheart Television International Inc.
P.O. Box 2030
Media, PA 19063

▶ Photographs

Official BBC stills from the show are available by mail from Whomobilia. Over three hundred are currently on their list, at a very reasonable price and in various different sizes.

Whomobilia
88 Rosebank
Holyport Road
London SW6 6LJ
England